★
Women
IN THE
White
House

A TARGET BOOK

Women *
IN THE
* White
House

FOUR
FIRST LADIES
★

Edited, with
commentary by
Bennett Wayne

GARRARD PUBLISHING COMPANY
CHAMPAIGN, ILLINOIS

Library of Congress Cataloging in Publication Data

Wayne, Bennett.
 Women in the White House.

 (Target)
 SUMMARY: Brief biographies of Martha Washington,
Abigail Adams, Dolly Madison, and Mary Lincoln.

 1. Washington, Martha Dandridge Custis, 1731-1802—
Juvenile literature. 2. Adams, Abigail Smith, 1744-1818
—Juvenile literature. 3. Madison, Dolley (Payne) Todd,
1768-1849—Juvenile literature. 4. Lincoln, Mary Todd,
1818-1882—Juvenile literature. [1. Washington, Martha
Dandridge Custis, 1731-1802. 2. Adams, Abigail Smith,
1744-1818. 3. Madison, Dolley (Payne) Todd, 1768-1849.
4. Lincoln, Mary Todd, 1818-1882. 5. Presidents—
Wives] I. Title.

E1762.W38   973'.0992 [B] [920]   75-20388
ISBN 0-8116-4915-6

Picture credits:

The Bettmann Archive: pp. 71, 118, 123, 148, 159, 162
Brown Brothers: pp. 24, 29, 53, 101, 110, 133
Culver Pictures: pp. 41, 120, 151 (both)
Fort Ticonderoga Collection, Fort Ticonderoga Museum, Ticonderoga,
 New York: p. 36
Kennedy Galleries, New York: p. 83
Library of Congress: pp. 48-49, 142, 150, 154
Massachusetts Historical Society: p. 58 (both)
The Metropolitan Museum of Art: p. 16
The Metropolitan Museum of Art, Rogers Fund, 1942: p. 92
National Gallery of Art: p. 44
National Gallery of Art, Edgar William and Bernice Garbisch Collection:
 p. 65
New York State Historical Association, Cooperstown, New York: p. 77
Pennsylvania Academy of the Fine Arts: p. 87
Virginia Historical Society: p. 107
Virginia State Library: p. 115
Washington and Lee University: pp. 9, 21

Contents

Women in the White House

In this picture Mrs. Gerald Ford, wife of the 38th president of the United States, is meeting with reporters. Their questions cover many subjects. They want to know what she thinks about important events. They want to know all about the First Family too. Mrs. Ford answers the reporters' questions graciously. She considers press conferences to be part of the work of a First Lady.

First Ladies are not elected to office. Nor are they given special duties by law. Still, they have shared many of the responsibilities of the presidency. They have not always had to face an army of reporters. But they have been expected to do many other things. First Ladies have entertained an unceasing parade of visitors to the White House. They have traveled with the president to near places and far. Often they have traveled alone as the president's representative. Always in the spotlight, they have been expected to be, above all, a shining example for all Americans.

This book is about four First Ladies—Martha Washington, Abigail Adams, Dolly Madison, and Mary Todd Lincoln. Not all of them won the admiration of the American people. Each in her own way, however, tried to meet the test of an exciting, but often trying, job.

This is a book about four president's wives, but more than that, a book about four women who occupy their own special place in history.

MARTHA WASHINGTON
1731-1802

Martha Custis was a young widow with
two small children when she first met
George Washington. The tall, pleasant
man who would one day be her husband was then a colonel in the Virginia
forces. But in time he would become
General Washington, commander in
chief of the Continental Army, and
then President Washington, the new
nation's first chief of state. Martha's
girlhood on a Virginia plantation and
her young womanhood in Williamsburg
had prepared her well for her life with
George Washington. She shared the
hardships of army-camp life during the
bitter winters of the Revolutionary War.
She served both as the president's
hostess and as his helpmate in the
early days of the United States. As
the very first First Lady, Martha
Washington was a model and an in-
spiration for the First Ladies who
followed her.

Martha Washington

First Lady of the Land

by LaVere Anderson

1. A Girl of Virginia

"Bessie, do squirrels like grape jelly?" Martha Dandridge asked.

Bessie, the cook, laughed. "Miss Martha, that pet squirrel of yours will like anything you give her."

"I'll take her some jelly when it is ready and see whether she does," Martha said. "Oh, this kettle is hot!"

"Be careful, child," the kindly black woman said. "Don't stand so close to the fire when you stir that jelly. What would your mama say if I let you get burned?"

Martha stepped back from the open fireplace, where a kettle hung over the flames. From the big pot came the sweet smell of grapes. Martha liked to cook. On this early fall morning in 1742, Bessie was teaching her to make grape jelly.

They were in the kitchen of Chestnut Grove. This was the farm, or plantation, in Virginia where Martha had been born in 1732. The family lived in a big white house. Behind it stood small houses for the slaves. Beyond were green fields of tobacco. Martha's father, John Dandridge, raised tobacco and shipped it to England.

Virginia plantations were far apart. People met at church on Sundays, and sometimes there were big parties. But Martha had little chance to play with other girls her own age. For company she had her three brothers and two baby sisters. She and her brothers liked to race their horses over the fields. Sometimes the boys took her boating or fishing on the Pamunkey River.

Martha's days were filled with lessons. Her mother taught her to sew and to "keep house." Her father taught her to read, write, and spell. There were few schools for children then, so each family taught its own children.

Of all her lessons, Martha liked cooking the best. Now she lifted the spoon from the big pot. Purple juice fell from the spoon. "Isn't it a pretty color, Bessie!"

Bessie nodded. "It looks ready to put into jars."

Soon the jelly jars were all filled. Martha took off her apron. "Oh, dear," she said. "It's time to study my spelling. I wish spelling were as much fun as cooking."

Bessie's big laugh filled the kitchen. "You are a born cook, Miss Martha. Don't forget to take some jelly to your squirrel."

Martha had made friends with a gray squirrel that came to her bedroom window. She had named it Maybelle.

In her sunny bedroom Martha sat at the desk with her spelling book. She heard a sound at the window. There was Maybelle! Martha opened the window a little and laid a spoon of jelly on the sill.

Maybelle sniffed at it. She took a little taste. She looked at Martha and clicked her teeth.

Martha smiled. "I know. You are saying, 'Martha Dandridge, don't you *ever* have any nuts?'"

Maybelle took a last taste of jelly. Then with a flick of her tail, she waved good-bye.

Martha turned again to her spelling lesson. *Scissors.* She looked hard at the word. All those letters *s*. She counted them. Four!

"How will I ever remember where they all go?" she thought. Then she had a happier thought. "Perhaps it won't matter if I am not a good speller. When I grow up, I will never need to spell except in letters to my family. The family won't mind if a word is wrong.

"It is not as if I will ever know important people like generals and governors. I will never have to write to *them*."

She bent over her spelling book once more. "S-c-i-s-s-o-r-s," she began.

2. The Governor's Ball

Five years passed quickly for busy Martha.

One bright morning she stood before the mirror in her bedroom. She smiled. The girl in the mirror smiled back.

"No!" Martha said aloud. "That was too big a grin. People will think I am silly."

She smiled again. Then she shook her head. "That one was not big enough. I will look as if I am cross. Oh, I wish I did not have to go to the governor's ball. I've never been to such a big party before. I won't know how to act."

Each year the governor of Virginia gave a great party. It was held in the governor's palace at Williamsburg, the capital city of Virginia. All the important plantation families were asked. Now that Martha was fifteen, she was invited too.

Martha began to walk slowly up and down her room. Her father had said that young ladies should walk slowly in a ballroom.

"Take short steps," she told herself. "Hold your head high. Smile."

Then she bent her knees to curtsy. She would have to curtsy to the governor.

Lower and lower Martha bowed. Suddenly she lost her balance and—KER-PLUNK! She fell to the floor.

Her mother came into the room. "Martha! Why are you sitting on the floor?"

Martha stood up. "I bowed too low and fell. Mama, must I go?"

"Of course you must go. You will be presented to the governor and his lady. Papa and I will be proud of you."

A few weeks later Martha and her parents went to Williamsburg. They stayed at an inn. There they met many friends who had also come to the party.

"I think everybody in Virginia wants to go to the governor's ball," Martha said to herself. "Everybody but me. I am sure to do something wrong."

The governor of Virginia was an Englishman sent to America by George II, king of Great Britain. Two nations—England and Scotland—were joined together in his kingdom. Virginia belonged to Great Britain and was one of her thirteen American colonies. But these colonies had been settled by Englishmen, so most of the colonists still thought of England as the "mother country."

On the night of the party, the governor's palace was lighted by hundreds of candles. Men and women in fine clothes filled the great ballroom. At one end of the room sat the governor and his lady.

A man called the names of people who were to

be presented to them. One by one these people walked down the long room to bow before the pair. Martha's heart beat with fear as she waited.

"MISS MARTHA DANDRIDGE."

"Your turn," Martha's father said. He gave her a little push. "Go along, my dear."

"Walk slowly," Martha told herself. "Head high. Smile."

It seemed a very long way to the end of the room. Her knees began to shake. Now she must curtsy. Suppose she fell the way she had at home?

She looked up at the governor and his lady. Her eyes grew wide with surprise. They looked so friendly!

Suddenly Martha was not afraid anymore. She dipped low in a beautiful curtsy.

When she stood up, she took five steps backward, as her father had told her to do. Then she turned and went back to her parents. She walked slowly, but she was so happy she felt like skipping.

"Well done, my girl," John Dandridge said. "I am proud of you."

Soon it was time for dancing to the music of violins. Many young men asked Martha to dance. They liked the pretty girl in the white dress, with her pink cheeks and shining brown hair.

One of the men was older than the others. His name was Daniel Parke Custis. He was in his thirties. Martha thought he had the kindest face she had ever seen. He asked her to dance. Then he asked her again. He brought her fruit and cake from the supper table. When the ball was over, he helped her into the Dandridge carriage.

"Well, Martha, Mr. Custis seems to like you very much," John Dandridge said as they drove back to the inn.

Martha's eyes sparkled. "Oh, papa—mama—," said the happy girl. "I'm so glad that we came to the governor's ball!"

Martha lived on a plantation much like the one above. Included are shops, fields, and slave quarters.

3. Mistress Custis

During the next three years, Daniel Parke Custis often visited Chestnut Grove. Pretty Martha and quiet, kindly Daniel fell in love.

"Why don't they marry?" people asked. "Martha is seventeen now and old enough to get married."

"Daniel's father has found fault with every girl Daniel has known," others answered. "His father is old. Daniel does not want to marry against his wishes and make him unhappy."

One day Martha and her mother were visiting friends in Williamsburg. They met Daniel's father there.

Old Mr. Custis had never seen Martha before. Now he looked hard at this girl his son loved. He saw that she had a sweet face and a gentle manner. They talked together. Like Daniel, old Mr. Custis lost his heart to Martha.

On a summer day in 1749, Martha became Mistress Daniel Parke Custis.

Daniel was a rich man and owned many farms. He and Martha lived on a big tobacco plantation in a beautiful house called the White House. Martha ran her home well.

"I am proud of my smart wife," Daniel told her one afternoon at dinner. On Virginia plantations the main meal of the day was usually in mid-afternoon.

"Mama taught me to keep house," Martha said. "And dear old Bessie taught me to cook. But no matter how hard papa tried, he never could teach me to spell."

Daniel laughed. "I can spell, but I could never make a spice cake like this one!" He took a big bite of the cake. "After such a fine dinner, I feel like taking a walk. Let's hunt for wild flowers in the woods."

Sometimes Daniel's business took him to Williamsburg. Martha always went with him. There they lived in Daniel's town house, called Six Chimneys. It was not far from the governor's palace.

Life in Williamsburg was exciting for Martha. People from all the great Virginia plantations came there to visit and shop. Daniel was a good friend of the governor, and he and Martha were invited to the governor's parties. In turn, they gave many parties. Martha wore beautiful dresses and jewels. Her carriage was one of the handsomest in all Williamsburg.

One day in 1755, Daniel came home from a visit with the governor. Martha was playing with their one-year-old son, Jacky.

Daniel smiled at the baby, but his eyes were grave.

"I have bad news," he told Martha. "The war

in the west is not going well. General Braddock's soldiers were beaten, and the general was killed."

"How dreadful!" Martha cried.

Great Britain and France were fighting over the rich Ohio Valley. Both said they owned it. Both had sent their soldiers to build forts and hold the land. Many Virginia men fought beside the British soldiers. General Braddock had been their commander.

"How did it happen?" Martha asked.

"The Indians were helping the French and taught them how to fight from behind trees. General Braddock was used to fighting in the open and did not understand this kind of warfare. Many of our soldiers were killed. When the general himself was wounded, a young Virginian took command. He is a colonel named George Washington.

"It is said he was very brave. Two horses were shot from under him. Yet he kept our soldiers together. If it had not been for him, more of our men would have died."

"Colonel Washington must be a fine man," Martha said.

Although the war in the west went on, it seemed far away to Martha when she and Daniel returned to their quiet plantation. In time Jacky had a little sister. She was called Patsy.

Then Daniel became ill. Doctors said his heart

was weak. Martha nursed him carefully and cooked special soups and puddings for him. She sat with him day and night. Still he grew worse.

On a hot afternoon in July 1757, Daniel died. He left his fortune to Martha. She was only 25, with two small children. For their sake she put on a brave smile.

She got them a puppy and baked sugar cookies for tea parties. Yet she did not feel brave. It frightened her to think of running the plantation and raising the children alone. And she missed Daniel dreadfully. She felt lost in the big house without him.

4. Colonel George Washington

"Dinner is almost ready. Richard should be home from town soon," Mistress Chamberlayne said. She smiled at her guest.

It had been many months since Daniel died. Martha was visiting her friends, the Chamberlaynes, at their plantation near Williamsburg. Jacky, four years old, and Patsy, two, were with her. Martha would not go anywhere without her children.

Mistress Chamberlayne looked out the window again for her husband. Down the road came men on horseback. "Here he is. He has somebody with him—somebody in an army uniform. Why, it is

Colonel George Washington

Colonel George Washington! How very nice that
Richard has brought him home."

Soon Martha was introduced to the brave soldier
Daniel had told her about. He was so tall that she
only came to his shoulder. For four years George
Washington had been fighting in the west. Now he
was commander in chief of the Virginia soldiers.
He had come back to Williamsburg for a short
time on army business.

Martha and George liked each other at once.
After dinner they sat in the parlor talking
together.

She told him about her life at the White House.

He told her about his plantation on the Potomac River. It was called Mount Vernon. Martha learned that she and George were the same age. His father, like hers, had been a tobacco planter.

"When the war is over, I am going back to Mount Vernon and farm the land," he said. "I hope I will never have to leave there again."

Martha smiled. This young officer was the hero of Virginia—a great soldier and leader of men. Yet what he really wanted to be was a farmer!

It was growing dark when George got up to say good-bye.

"No, indeed, Colonel Washington," said Richard Chamberlayne when he found his guest ready to go. "Nobody leaves my house after sunset. You must stay the night."

That evening George sat on the floor and played with Jacky and Patsy. He liked the children, and they made friends with him at once. They seemed to think he was a big new toy.

Next morning George rode away. Martha had invited him to visit the White House. Soon he came for a visit. He came to see Martha every chance he got. He and Martha fell in love. George, as well as Martha, had been very lonely. He looked forward to having a family at Mount Vernon.

"We will be married as soon as I can leave the army," George told Martha. "It would be wrong for me to leave my command while the Ohio Valley is still in danger."

It was winter before the British began to win the long war. The French left the Ohio Valley. At last George felt free to marry.

How busy the White House was on January 6, 1759! George and Martha were married there that evening.

Soft light from candles and open fires shone on the many guests all dressed in their fine clothes. The governor and his lady were present. Tables were spread with beautiful silver and dishes.

George looked very handsome in blue knee breeches and a coat lined with red silk. Martha was lovely in a yellow dress, with pearls in her hair. She wore high-heeled silk slippers, because George was so tall. Proud and happy, she stood beside him.

Jacky and Patsy watched while their mother was married to their new father. Then there was a fine feast. Jacky enjoyed it all, but Patsy fell asleep eating her cake.

5. The Farmer's Wife

A coach pulled by four horses rolled down the long curved drive. Inside sat George and Martha Washington with the children and their nurse.

At Mount Vernon Martha and the children greet
George after a hunt.

"Whoa!" the coachman called out. The horses stopped.

George turned to Martha. "Welcome home, my dear," he said. "This is Mount Vernon."

Martha looked out at a square two-story house. Its white paint gleamed in the afternoon sun. New glass sparkled in the windows. Below the big lawn she could see the blue waters of the Potomac River.

"It's beautiful!" she cried.

George looked pleased. "There is a lot of work waiting to be done, though. I have been away so long that things have run down. The barns and fences need fixing. The fields must be cleared. I want to plant wheat and corn as well as tobacco. I must plant more flowers, and grass, and fruit trees too. You can see I am going to be a very busy farmer."

"And the farmer's wife is going to help too," Martha laughed.

She did help George. Her days started at sunrise. With a bunch of keys hanging from her belt, she went to unlock the storeroom. There she gave out the day's food to the cook.

Often there were guests for breakfast. In colonial Virginia, towns were far apart, and there were few inns. Travelers spent the night at the homes of friends along the way. George ate a small breakfast—corncakes, honey, and coffee. But guests liked ham and eggs, fried apples, and fresh fish.

During the day the mistress of Mount Vernon had much to do. There were many slaves, but they needed to be trained.

Martha taught the women how to spin yarn from wool. Then she showed them how to weave the yarn into cloth. It was a rough cloth called "homespun."

She taught both men and women how to make wine, perfume, powder, and medicines. These could be ordered from England. But it took time for slow ships to cross the ocean.

George was busy too. He looked after the outside work. Mount Vernon had its own carpenters, and men to lay bricks and to shoe horses.

There were many fields to plant. There were cows to be milked and sheep to be sheared for their wool.

There was fun as well as work. Friends and family often came to visit. Everybody liked George and small, cheerful Martha. She became known as a fine hostess and a wonderful cook.

She and George went visiting too. There were hunting parties, dances, and dinners. On Sundays they drove nine miles to church.

Each fall and spring they went to Williamsburg, when the House of Burgesses met there. The burgesses were a group of Virginians who made most of the laws for the colony.

George had been elected a burgess in 1758, and he was reelected time after time. He became one of the most important members. When he spoke, the other burgesses listened carefully.

Wherever George and Martha went, they took the children. George was a loving father. He gave both of the children fat ponies to ride. He gave Patsy a harpsichord, an instrument that looked very much like a piano.

Pretty Patsy often sat at the harpsichord in the candlelight and played music for her father.

Jacky was a good-natured boy, but he would not study. All he cared about was having fun. George hired a teacher, Mr. Walter MacGowan, for him. The teacher could seldom find his pupil at lesson time. Jacky was off training his dogs to hunt fox. When Jacky was fourteen, George said he must go away to a boys' school.

It was hard for Martha to see her son go away, but she tried to be cheerful. Tears would have upset Patsy. Patsy was not well, and Martha was worried about her.

As the years passed, the lovely girl grew thin and pale. Many doctors were called in, and Patsy was given all kinds of medicine. Sometimes she seemed to be better. It was at those times that

Martha's laughter rang through the house. Yet soon Patsy would be ill again.

One summer day in 1773, Patsy died. She was only seventeen. Jacky, nineteen now, came home from school to stay. His mother needed him.

Jacky still didn't like books. He liked horses and dogs—and Nelly Calvert. She was a girl he had known for a year, and she had often visited at Mount Vernon. When Christmas came, Martha and George gave her the Christmas presents they had ordered for Patsy from England. In time, Jacky and Nelly were married.

Martha did not go to the wedding. She still missed Patsy too much.

"I would cry and spoil everything," she said.

Instead, she wrote a loving letter. "My dear Nelly—God took from me a daughter when June roses were blooming. He has given me another daughter about her age when winter winds are blowing, to warm my heart again."

Jacky brought pretty, merry Nelly to live at Mount Vernon. Slowly Martha learned to smile once more.

6. War Clouds

Martha sat quietly at her dinner table while the four men talked.

George and Martha's guests were important men in the House of Burgesses. George had asked them to dinner on this spring day in 1774.

Suddenly a word rang loud in Martha's ears. War!

Her hand began to shake. She laid down her fork.

Why, George's friends were saying the American colonies might go to war with Great Britain!

She began to listen carefully. Soon she understood. It was the old quarrel about taxes. In 1765 the new king, George III, had tried to make the

George and Martha's peaceful life at Mount Vernon was threatened by war with Great Britain.

colonies pay taxes on goods from England. The colonists refused.

They told the king, "We are free men and cannot be taxed against our wishes." They told him Great Britain had no right to make any laws for them. The king said that Great Britain did have that right.

The colonists got around the tax by ordering few things from England. Women wore homespun dresses. Men did without new guns and saddles. Then the king stopped most of the taxes. Martha had hoped the trouble was over. Now—*war*?

She looked at George. There were new lines in his face.

"He is worried," she thought. "He has not told me because I have been so sad about Patsy. I must forget my own feelings and help him."

The men began to talk about trouble in Boston. Last December some men in Massachusetts had dumped 342 big boxes of English tea into Boston harbor. They had been angry because a new tax had been put on the tea. The king punished Boston by closing its harbor to trade. No ships could get in or out. He sent British soldiers to take over the city.

Now one of the burgesses said, "Massachusetts men are ready to fight the British soldiers. Virginia must raise an army to help her."

"If King George can close a Massachusetts harbor," said another man, "he will soon be closing Virginia harbors. If he can send his army to Boston, he can send it to Williamsburg. We may have to fight the British soldiers."

"You are right," a burgess said. "Massachusetts' fight is Virginia's fight too. All the colonies must stand together. Besides the tax laws, Great Britain has made other laws which we do not like. She has taken freedoms from all of us."

"Perhaps the matter can be settled peacefully," George said. "At least, we must try."

They did try. Leading men from twelve of the thirteen colonies met together in Philadelphia, Pennsylvania in 1774. This meeting was called the Continental Congress. George was one of the men sent from Virginia to the Congress. They wrote a long letter to the king. It said the colonies had a right to govern themselves. The king paid no attention to the letter.

In all the colonies, young men began marching and drilling. In Massachusetts British soldiers were fired upon at a bridge near Concord. The British had been trying to take away the colonists' gunpowder that was hidden there. By late spring 1775, fighting had begun in other parts of New England too.

Another meeting of Congress was called. Again

George traveled to Philadelphia. When he left home this time, he was wearing an army uniform. The sight made Martha shiver in the warm May air.

"Does he think it will be a long war?" she wondered. She did not worry him with her fears. The best way to help him was to send him away with a smile.

One day a letter came to Mount Vernon from George in Philadelphia. Tears rolled down Martha's cheeks as she read it.

"My dearest—," it began. It said that he had been made commander of the Continental army. He was leaving at once for Massachusetts.

He wrote: "I would find more happiness in one month with you at Mount Vernon than in fifty years of war. But the American cause is being put in my care."

Martha folded the letter and put it into her pocket. She wiped away her tears. "A general's wife does not cry!" she told herself.

General Washington! How strange that sounded to her ears. She was not surprised he had been chosen. He would make a fine general, she knew. Virginia was the largest of the thirteen colonies, and he was Virginia's best soldier.

But General Washington would need the help of every American. How could she help? Her eyes fell on a basket that sat on a nearby table. The basket held her knitting needles and some wool. "Yes," thought Martha, "that will help."

The general's wife picked up the needles and began to knit a pair of socks for her general.

"I'll knit many pairs for him," she told herself. "His feet will never get cold no matter how deep the snow is in Massachusetts."

7. A Nation Is Born

The British governor of Virginia was angry because the colonists had taken up arms against the king. He was especially angry at General Washington. The governor said he would send a gunboat up the Potomac River. Soldiers would burn the general's home and take Mistress Washington prisoner.

Martha was not afraid. All the same, she made sure that Mount Vernon's treasures were safe. She packed the fine silver and dishes into barrels.

"If trouble comes, we will hide the barrels in the barns," she told Lund Washington, "and then escape." Lund was George's cousin. He had come to take care of Mount Vernon while George was away at war.

At Christmas Martha visited George in faraway Massachusetts. The general's army was in winter camp outside Boston. George wrote that he had been given a comfortable house to live in. There was little fighting in the winter months. He was homesick for her. Would she come?

"I must start at once," Martha cried. "Jacky and Nelly must come too. George needs us."

Quickly she filled her coach with good things to eat from Mount Vernon's big storeroom. She packed nuts and apples, hams, jelly, and fruitcake. There was hardly room left in the coach for people to sit.

It was a long hard trip over rough, icy roads. But how happy George was to see her! How the lonely soldiers enjoyed the Christmas food she brought!

Martha mended George's clothes and looked after the sick. She knit socks for the soldiers. When guns boomed, she knit faster. Nobody knew how the gunfire frightened her.

In the spring George was ready to attack the British in Boston. To his surprise the British did not stand and fight. They marched onto their ships in Boston harbor and sailed away. Washington's army got ready to move on to New York.

Soon after George arrived in New York, Martha joined him there. George worried about her because he believed the British would attack there soon. Finally he decided that she should go home.

"You must stop at Philadelphia, where you will be safe," George told Martha. "Stay there until we can be sure the governor will not attack Mount Vernon."

Martha went to Philadelphia.

The Continental Congress was there too. At this meeting the Congress was working on a very great paper—the Declaration of Independence. The Declaration said the American colonies were free from Great Britain. They were a new and independent nation, the United States of America. Congress was ready to take a vote to approve the Declaration.

It was very hot in Philadelphia on the summer afternoon Martha visited her friend Dolly Hancock. Dolly's husband, John, was the president of the Congress.

The two ladies sat in Dolly's parlor, fanning themselves and talking. Outside, people were walking past the windows toward the State House, where Congress met. Martha and Dolly knew a crowd was gathered there, waiting to hear about the vote.

Suddenly the bell in the State House began to ring. DING—DONG—DING—DONG—. The Declaration had been approved!

To the people outside, it was a time for celebration. But the two women in the parlor

The reading of the Declaration of Independence was an event Martha would always remember.

thought of their husbands. John Hancock was president of the Congress that had just passed the Declaration. George Washington led the army that fought Great Britain. If America lost the war and the two men were caught, they would be tried for treason to the king. They would be hanged. Their wives knew it well.

But they were brave women. They tried to smile as the bell rang out.

"A new nation has been born," Dolly said.

"On July 4, 1776! It will be a day to remember," said Martha.

Four days later, July 8, Martha listened to a public reading of the Declaration in the State

House yard. Then the State House bell rang again, and all the bells in the city sounded. A great crowd gathered to hear the words of the Declaration. People fired guns and built bonfires in the streets. They cheered and cried for joy.

"The United States of America!" they shouted. What a grand name that was!

8. Winter at Valley Forge

It was almost dark when Martha's coach drove up to Valley Forge one cold day in February 1778. Washington's soldiers were stationed there in Pennsylvania for the winter. How lonely the valley looked with the snow-covered hills closing it in.

The coach stopped in front of a small stone farmhouse. Martha knew this must be the command post where George lived. In the distance, she could see long rows of log huts.

A door opened. There, in the candlelight, stood the general. He hurried to her.

Once again, Martha had come to visit George, her coach filled with food from home. This would be her third winter in camp. "I do not want you with me during the summer, when there is heavy fighting," George had told her. So she spent her summers at Mount Vernon. It was safe there now that the governor had gone back to England.

"George looks so much older," Martha thought as the two sat talking that night. "It is because the war has not gone well."

The Americans had won a few battles. But General Washington's small army had lost New York, and the British had captured Philadelphia. Congress had fled to Baltimore, Maryland. Martha tried to think of some cheerful news.

"Jacky and Nelly's new baby is a dear. Everything is fine at home, and I am glad to be back with you."

"Wait until you see this camp," George said. "You may not want to stay."

"What is wrong, George?"

"Our men have no warm clothes and little food. They do not even have clean straw to sleep on. They built huts because our tents leaked. It is very cold inside those huts, and there are few blankets. Some men sit up all night by the campfires to keep from freezing. Many are sick, but we have no medicines."

His voice grew loud as the sad and angry words went on.

"Martha, there are 10,000 soldiers in this camp. At least 3,000 of them are unfit for duty because they have no shoes or coats. There is not a cow to kill for food. We have only 25 barrels of flour to feed the whole army!"

Martha's face grew grave. "What can you do?"

"Write more letters to Congress," George said. "I must beg for food and shoes and medicine. Yet I know that Congress has little money, and war costs a great deal."

"Then things could not be worse?" Martha asked.

"Of course they could!" A proud look came into George's eyes. "The men could run off and go home, but they do not. They stay because they believe in freedom. They are patriots. England can never defeat such men as these!"

The next morning Martha walked down the street of log huts. She saw many soldiers huddled around their little campfires. They were thin and sick and dressed in pieces of torn uniforms. Some had wrapped rags around their bare feet. There were bloody footprints in the snow where they had walked.

Every man stood up as the general's wife passed by. "Good day to you, Lady Washington," they said. "Welcome to Valley Forge."

Love shone from Martha's eyes for these young men who stood so straight. They might look like scarecrows, but they behaved like the fine soldiers they were.

The young soldiers were to see their general's lady many times in the cold dark days to come.

She went back and forth to the camp hospital, an officer walking beside her. He carried a big pot of hot soup she had made for the sick.

Martha met the wives of other officers who had come to be with their husbands.

"Let us form a sewing group," she told them. "We can mend the soldiers' clothes and make socks for them." All the ladies were glad to help.

George's birthday came. He was 46 on February 22, 1778. Martha found some tough old hens and cooked them until they were tender for his birthday dinner.

The cruel winter dragged on. Often the soldiers drilled long hours with the snow flying in their faces. Valley Forge was only 25 miles from Philadelphia. On a clear day the cold and hungry Americans could see the city from their camp. They knew the British soldiers there were warm and well fed.

One day a tall, laughing French soldier came to Valley Forge. His name was Lafayette, and he was nineteen years old. He was so interested in the Americans' ideas about freedom that he had come to join Washington's army.

Lafayette was an important nobleman in his own country. He knew that the American government had asked France to help the new nation in its war with England.

Martha shared the long, cruel winter at Valley Forge
with George and his loyal soldiers.

"I will also ask the French king to send ships and money," he promised.

It did not take the merry young officer long to win the hearts of Martha and George. George came to look upon him almost as a son. He called Lafayette "the French boy."

So the winter passed. The snow melted, and the grass grew green. On the hills pink and white dogwood flowered. The air was warm and sweet. Word came that France would help the Americans fight the British. How the soldiers cheered that news!

"We will celebrate," said the general. "We will have a parade."

The soldiers were thin. Their clothes were patched. But they polished their guns and put flowers in their hats. In the bright spring sunshine they marched, heads high. The camp band played every tune it knew, and then started all over again.

To Martha it was a wonderful sight. She could tell by George's face that he was proud and happy too. The terrible winter of Valley Forge was past.

With France's help, the war would be won. George was right, she realized. England could never defeat such men as these!

In time the Americans did win the war, but it

took five more years. Martha spent part of every winter with George, wherever he was. She sewed, knit, and cooked for the sick. She was always helpful and cheerful, and nobody ever heard her complain. Even when Jacky joined the army and died of camp fever, Martha did not let anyone see her tears. The soldiers all liked the general's lady. They said she did her part to help win the war.

9. Home to Mount Vernon

It was Christmas Eve, 1783, at Mount Vernon.

The sweet smell of bayberry candles filled the rooms. Evergreens hung from the walls. In the kitchen the cook was busy making a Christmas feast. Everybody was happy, and Martha was the happiest of all. General Washington had just come home from the war!

There were children to welcome him.

"Merry Christmas, grandpapa!" cried little Nelly.

"Mer-ry Criss-mus!" shouted her small brother George.

George lifted them up and hugged them. Martha watched with a loving smile.

They were her grandchildren. Jacky and Nelly had had four children. After Jacky died, Nelly married again and went to live with her new husband. The two youngest children stayed behind.

Martha and George adopted them. Dark-haired little Nelly was four now. Her brother George was almost two. He had been named for George Washington. People called him "Little Washington" and sometimes "Mr. Tub."

George was glad to be home, the war over and won. Soon after Christmas he began to make plans for Mount Vernon.

"We will raise more turkeys, geese, pigs, sheep, cows, horses, and mules," he told Martha. "That means we must build another barn. We must add more rooms to the house, too, and plant more trees and flowers. We will make Mount Vernon one of the finest plantations in Virginia."

The Washington Family by Edward Savage

"I can see we will be busy," Martha laughed.

One summer day George got a present. His friend Lafayette sent him seven giant hunting dogs from France. They were very fierce. Everyone was afraid of them except George and Mr. Tub. By now the little boy was four. He wanted to ride horses like his grandpa, but a horse was too big for him. One morning a stableboy ran to the house to find Martha and George.

"Mr. Tub is with Vulcan!" cried the frightened boy. "That mean old dog got out of his pen. He'll *bite* Mr. Tub!"

Martha's face turned white. She and George ran to the stable. Suddenly they stopped, and George began to laugh.

There was Vulcan, walking slowly around the yard. On his broad back sat Mr. Tub. Vulcan was just the right size for a little boy to ride, and Vulcan liked playing horse!

Vulcan was put back into his pen. Mr. Tub was scolded.

"No more dog-riding!" Martha told him while George still laughed.

Mount Vernon was always full of guests. Some of them stayed for weeks. Martha and George seldom sat down to a meal alone. George told a friend, "I have 101 cows, but I still have to buy butter to feed all our guests."

Among the guests were men from Congress. They were worried about the new nation. Each state made its own laws and had its own leaders. The men said that Congress did not have enough power to govern the country.

"We need a better government," they said. "We need a Congress that has more power, and there should be one man to lead all the states."

Martha grew fearful. Would they ask George to be the leader? She hoped not. She knew he did not want to leave Mount Vernon again.

A meeting of men from all the states was held in Philadelphia. George was one of the delegates. The men planned for a strong new government and wrote a Constitution. They sent copies of the Constitution to the states for adoption. Then Congress met again to elect a president. He must be somebody all the people trusted. They elected George Washington.

10. The President's Wife

Martha stood at the front door of the crowded room. It was the parlor of the president's mansion in New York City, the nation's first capital. "So many people waiting to meet us!" she thought.

She was giving her first party as the wife of the president. She wanted to make George proud. She wasn't sure she could. "How does a president's wife act?" she wondered. There was nobody to ask. Suddenly Martha remembered another important party a long time ago. "Walk slowly," somebody had said. "Head high. Smile."

"Of course!" thought Martha. "Papa!"

Slowly the president's wife walked through the door, head high, smiling.

It was a fine party. George moved among the guests, greeting each one. Martha sat on a sofa and talked to many people. They all liked friendly Mistress Washington.

So Martha's life as the First Lady began that spring of 1789. The nation had never had a First Lady before. She had to make her own rules. George, as the first president of the United States, had to make his own rules too.

George knew that as president he would set the example for presidents to come. This worried him. How could he be sure that he would act wisely and set the right example?

"I am just a farmer and a soldier," he told Martha.

"You are a *president!*" she said.

Martha was glad when the capital was moved from New York to Philadelphia. She felt more at home there. She went to balls, dinners, and theater parties. She took the children on shopping trips. She wrote long letters to friends. Sometimes she had to stop and think about a word. Then she smiled and said to herself:

"Martha Dandridge, you should have studied your spelling. Maybe you aren't writing to generals and governors, but you are writing to their wives!"

Martha did not care for public life. She counted

Martha Washington, the first First Lady of the Land, receives guests at a glittering reception.

the days until George's four years as president
would be over.

George had been a good president, but the new
nation was still weak. It still needed a strong man
like George to lead it. He was elected for another
four-year term.

Martha tried hard to hide her disappointment.

Head high, smiling, she went to the balls and dinners. She did not forget she was the president's wife. She wrote a friend:

> The dearest wish of my heart is to go back to Mount Vernon. Yet I cannot blame George for obeying the voice of his country.

Slowly the years passed. They were hard ones for George. England and France were at war again. Spain was making trouble for the United States. Some of the states quarreled among themselves. There was little money to run the government. But somehow George kept the nation on its feet.

One morning cannon fire awakened Martha. It sounded like Valley Forge again. She jumped out of bed.

"What is happening?" she cried.

Martha soon found out. It was February 22, 1796, and Americans were celebrating George Washington's 64th birthday. Church bells rang, and all day people came to the president's house to wish him well. Martha had punch and cake ready for everyone. In the evening there was a big party, with music and dancing.

At last the four years were over. George was

asked to serve a third term. "No," he said. "It is time for another man." John Adams, the vice-president, was elected president.

Martha and George returned to Mount Vernon. Nelly went with them, but her brother stayed at school.

Mount Vernon was beautiful as they drove toward it. The fresh green grass and first flowers of spring made home look like a fairyland to Martha.

"We'll never leave again," she said.

They had three happy years doing the things they loved best. Then on a winter day in 1799, George died after a short illness. Martha lived on at Mount Vernon. Friends and family came for long visits. They always found her cheerful. She missed George terribly, but she remembered what he had often said: "It is better to go laughing than crying through life."

On May 22, 1802, Martha died. She was almost 70 years old.

Americans honor George Washington as "The Father of His Country." Martha is honored too. She was a great and good lady, the first "First Lady of the Land."

ABIGAIL ADAMS
1744-1818

"Politics are as natural to me as breathing," Abigail Adams once said. And so was helping her husband, John Adams. Abigail spent lonely years rearing their four children and running the farm all by herself. Meanwhile, John helped the United States win its independence in the Revolutionary War. Then he went to Europe to make treaties with other countries. Abigail stayed behind to care for the family. It was almost nine years before she could join John in Europe. Still, she never lost faith in herself or the cause they both believed in. As ambassador's lady and later as president's wife, Abigail showed the same courage and good humor that had seen her through the years of loneliness.

Abigail Adams

"Dear Partner"

by Helen Stone Peterson

1. A Terrible Night

Eleven-year-old Abigail Smith awoke suddenly. It was before daybreak on November 18, 1755. The bed, shared with her older sister Mary, was shaking. The girls leaped from it and raced down the narrow stairs to the kitchen. The whole house was shaking!

Their mother stood in front of the fireplace, her face white. Their little sister Elizabeth clung to her mother and sobbed wildly. Their father was staring out the window. Abigail watched milk spill over the sides of a bowl on the tottering table.

"What's happening?" she cried.

Suddenly the milk stopped spilling. The house stopped shaking.

Abigail's father turned around. "We have had a terrible earthquake. I'm afraid it has done great damage."

A few minutes later he was hurrying out the door to see how things were in the town. He was the minister of the Congregational Church in Weymouth, Massachusetts. He also ran the farm where his family lived.

When he returned, he brought good news. "I don't think that anyone in Weymouth has been hurt. Some chimneys lost a few bricks. That seems to be all."

"What about William?" Mrs. Smith asked anxiously. Abigail's brother William was visiting his uncle in Boston, about twelve miles away.

Mr. Smith nodded. "The danger is greater in the city because of the many brick buildings. I'll ride there at once. And I'll stop at Mount Wollaston."

Grandmother and Grandfather Quincy lived in the big house at Mount Wollaston on the shore road. Abigail spent some of her happiest days with them in their beautiful mansion. The Quincys, her mother's parents, were one of the leading families in Massachusetts.

Massachusetts was an English colony and had an English governor. But the colonists made most of their own laws. Grandfather Quincy had been active in the government a long time. Abigail hated to think that he or grandmother might have been hurt.

"Come, girls," Mrs. Smith called to them after father had ridden off on his horse. "It's our duty to do the work we planned."

The girls had planned to make mince pies for Thanksgiving. Their mother was teaching them to cook and sew and spin and weave. "You must know these things so you can manage your own homes some day," she often told them. "Someday you will have your own families."

The girls worked well together. After the dough was mixed, Abigail rolled it lightly into crusts. But her thoughts turned to her father. "Oh, what will he find?"

When her work was done, Abigail slipped into the study and opened a book. She had been sickly as a small child and hadn't gone to school. She studied with her father instead. More than anything, she liked to read.

Abigail was reading when a carriage rolled into their driveway. "My grandparents have come! So the earthquake didn't hurt them!" Abigail cried. She ran to greet them.

Grandmother Quincy flung her arms around all three girls. "This is what I said last night:

I see the moon, the moon sees me
The moon sees three girls I want
to see!"

Abigail laughed softly.

Grandmother caught sight of the pies. She praised the girls. "Such fine golden crusts! We'll have a good Thanksgiving."

But Abigail wasn't sure. She was still worried.

Her grandparents stayed until father returned. "William is perfectly all right and so are the others," he reported.

Abigail felt a burst of happiness. Everyone in her family was safe! Now she was sure they would have a good Thanksgiving.

2. Partners for Life

It was a fine winter evening, not long after Abigail's seventeenth birthday. Her older sister Mary was expecting Richard Cranch. Mary was engaged to him.

There was a knock at the door. "Abigail, please let Richard in," called Mary. She was still in front of her mirror, and their mother was out.

Abigail opened the door, giving her deepest curtsy. "Welcome, Sir Richard," she said gaily. Then she saw that he wasn't alone. His friend John Adams was with him. Abigail blushed. She wished she had been more proper.

Mary appeared and took Richard into the parlor. Abigail's father invited John into his study. Then he asked Abigail to bring some apples.

Abigail had known John ever since she was a little girl. He lived on a farm in Braintree, four miles away. He had graduated from Harvard College and was getting started as a lawyer.

Abigail was nineteen years old when she and John posed for these companion portraits.

Abigail returned with a bowl of red apples. On top she had placed a big yellow pear. "It's from a tree that's over 100 years old," she explained.

John looked at Abigail in surprise. Most girls weren't interested in things like that. But he was interested in the fruit trees and everything else on his farm. His friends often called him Farmer John.

John was even more surprised when Abigail left the room, taking with her a book of Shakespeare's plays. Most girls didn't read books like that in their spare time. But John did.

John came back again. Before long he was calling on Abigail often.

Abigail's eyes grew bright with a new happiness. She was falling in love with John. And he was in love with her.

Abigail's mother frowned. She wanted the best for her daughter. John was from a good family, but not a leading one like the Quincys. Would he ever be anything more than a poor country lawyer? "Please wait," she said when they spoke of marriage.

So Abigail and John became engaged, and waited. Abigail had letters from John when he couldn't make his regular visits to her. "Dear partner of all my joys and sorrows," he wrote.

In time Abigail's mother saw that they knew their own hearts.

Abigail was married to John in 1764, just before her twentieth birthday. Her father read the wedding service. Afterward there was a wedding feast with grandparents, aunts, uncles, and cousins.

Abigail and John drove off before the feasting had ended. Their farmhouse in Braintree was waiting for them.

3. The Boston Massacre

Abigail hugged her baby. "Now I lay you down to sleep," she whispered as she put her little daughter in the cradle. The baby was named after her but was called Nabby.

Abigail's heart was full of happiness. She and John had been married one year. They had their darling baby. They had their small farmhouse, which Abigail loved. John's office was downstairs. His widowed mother lived next door.

Abigail's only worry was America's quarrel with England. Earlier that year England had passed a law ordering the colonies to pay a heavy tax. The Americans were angry. Leaders from the colonies were holding a meeting in New York.

"The tax is unfair because the colonists had no part in making that law," John had told Abigail. "It's our right to make our own laws. We cannot let our rights be taken from us."

John had written down his thoughts about the tax law. Abigail was proud when the newspaper in Boston printed John's words.

Abigail was lifting a golden corncake from the oven when she heard a noise. The next minute John bounded into the kitchen and swept her into his arms.

She saw that he was excited about something

important. But he stopped and kissed Nabby's soft cheek gently.

John spilled out his news to Abigail while they ate supper. "I've heard a report about the meeting in New York. The men there agreed that England has no right to tax us without our consent."

"What do you think will happen now?" asked Abigail.

"I think England will remove the tax," John replied.

"Will that end the quarrel between the colonies and England?"

John shook his head. "I don't know."

Early the next year England removed the hated tax. "But we are not giving up our right to make other laws for the colonies," the English rulers declared.

After Abigail read this in the newspaper, she knew the quarrel hadn't ended.

The months flew by. When Nabby was two years old, Abigail and John had their first son. They named him John Quincy after Abigail's grandfather.

Before Johnny had his first birthday, the family moved to Boston. John was becoming known as an excellent lawyer. More and more people were also turning to him for advice on government matters. He decided his office should be in the city.

By this time England had passed another law ordering the colonies to pay other taxes. Soldiers were sent to Boston to make sure that England's laws were obeyed.

Abigail listened to John's warning.

"These soldiers will surely keep our people stirred up. There is certain to be trouble!"

Sometimes boys threw oyster shells at the soldiers and called them bad names. In the second winter a terrible thing happened. John heard about it and hurried home to tell Abigail.

"The English soldiers have killed three of our men. Others are hurt, perhaps even dying."

Abigail's eyes flooded with tears.

"A mob of young men threw snowballs and chunks of ice at a soldier on duty," John continued. "Other soldiers came running to help him. In the uproar that followed, one of our hotheads tried to grab a gun from a soldier. The soldiers fired."

The next day John had something more to tell Abigail. "I have agreed to be the lawyer for the English soldiers. No other lawyer would take the case. One said he would help me, however."

"But John!" Abigail gasped, turning pale. "People say the English soldiers murdered our men. They're calling it a massacre."

"The law will decide whether it was murder or

self-defense," said John. "In Massachusetts a man has the right to a fair trial. It's my duty to help keep it that way."

"Yes," Abigail nodded. She saw how much courage John had. Some people would accuse him of siding with the English. "I'm proud of you," she said, kissing him.

At their trial the English soldiers were found not guilty of murder. As time passed, all Americans were proud that the soldiers had had a fair trial.

Abigail and John watched the quarrel between the colonies and England grow bigger. John moved his family back to the old farmhouse in Braintree, where they would be safer. There were two more children now, Charles and Tommy.

The family was together at the farm on April 19, 1775. A horse galloped down the road. Abigail and John heard the rider shout, "The English soldiers are fighting the Americans at Lexington and Concord!"

The Revolutionary War had begun.

4. Independence Day

Just two months later, on June 17, Abigail was awakened by the thunder of cannon. "What's happening?" she asked herself.

John was not at home. He was attending the

new Continental Congress meeting in Philadelphia, Pennsylvania. Men from all thirteen colonies were meeting to plan their country's future. They had sent pleas to England, "Let us keep our rights!" They were sending one more plea now.

Abigail dressed quickly. A few minutes later she was at the big fireplace, stirring cornmeal mush for breakfast.

"Where's the battle? Are we winning?" asked five-year-old Charles. Nabby, Johnny, and Tommy fixed their eyes on their mother's face.

"I don't know," Abigail answered them steadily.

They were finishing breakfast when a messenger came to the door. "Our men are trying hard to hold Bunker Hill in Charlestown! But the English ships are bombarding them with cannon!"

"Come," Abigail told her oldest son. She and seven-year-old Johnny climbed to the top of their own hill. Looking across Boston harbor they saw the flash of the thundering cannon.

Later black smoke darkened the sky. "The English are burning the homes and churches of Charlestown!" cried Abigail.

The Americans lost the battle, but they showed how bravely they could fight. Soon General George Washington arrived to lead the soldiers.

Farmers hurried to join his army. Abigail fed them when they stopped at her farmhouse. Women and children fled from Boston to safer places. Abigail fed them too. Food became scarce.

"We can eat huckleberries and milk," Abigail wrote to John.

English soldiers raided towns along the shore, stealing sheep and cows. Would they also raid Braintree? Would they set fire to Abigail's home and church?

"We fear them not!" Abigail wrote to John.

It was a deadly sickness that struck Braintree next. Abigail got well in time to take care of Tommy, who almost died. The maid, who helped

Abigail and Johnny looked across Boston harbor and saw gunfire on Bunker Hill at Charlestown.

Abigail, died. Abigail's mother came to help. She caught the sickness and died too.

"Oh, my bursting heart," Abigail wrote to John.

The awful winter passed. In March 1776, the English soldiers withdrew from Massachusetts. Now they would fight the Americans in New York and other places.

"It's time we cut all of our ties to England!" Abigail wrote to John. "I long to hear that the Congress has declared independence."

Abigail heard from John in July. "A resolution was passed that these united colonies are free and independent states." Abigail felt a rush of joy.

She called to her children. She read aloud the shining words John had written to her about Independence Day:

> It ought to be solemnized with pomp and parade, with shows, games, sports, guns, bells, bonfires, and illuminations from one end of this continent to the other, from this time forward for evermore.

5. "When is Papa Coming Home?"

Abigail had to manage the farm while John was away at the Continental Congress. Farm workers were scarce because the men had joined the army. "I believe I could gather corn and husk it, but I should make a poor figure at digging potatoes," she wrote to John.

Abigail was also her children's teacher. The schoolmasters had marched off to the army saying, "War's begun, school's done." Abigail taught French and Latin to Nabby and Johnny. And she taught Charles and Tommy to read and write.

Whenever she had a spare moment, Abigail sat down to her spinning wheel. No cloth was coming from England. Abigail and her maids had to spin and weave homemade cloth. "If we didn't, the children would be naked!" Abigail wrote to John.

The children kept asking, "When is papa coming home?"

One August day Abigail opened a letter from John. "I'm coming for a visit," he wrote. Smiling, Abigail read the letter to the children. Would Abigail send him a horse to ride home? he asked.

"What can I do?" Abigail thought. Their own horse was lame. Good horses were hard to find because the army had taken so many.

Suddenly Charles spoke up. "Mama, I want papa to come home. Take my dollar and get a horse for papa."

Abigail kissed her curly-haired boy. "Your father will come home. I promise."

Abigail's father sent his horse to John. But John had to put off his visit. Battles had started around New York City. The Americans were losing them. John was working hard to build a better army. His job was like that of today's secretary of defense.

At last, in October, another message came. Johnny jumped off his pony and ran into the house, carrying the letter. Several times a week now Johnny swung into his saddle and rode to Boston for the mail.

Abigail read the letter out loud. "I'm starting home," John wrote. Charles and Tommy cheered.

Later they were painting thirteen little stripes on the sleds they would use as soon as snow fell. While they worked, they chanted their favorite verse:

"The English king
Lost states thirteen!"

How delighted Abigail and all the children were when John reached home. Every day together was a happy one. Then after Christmas John rode away again to Congress.

Another long year dragged by. When John reached home the next winter, Abigail thought he would stay. He had served four years in Congress. He decided not to run for office again right away.

John was home just three weeks when a letter arrived from Congress. The United States wanted France to join the fight against England. Benjamin Franklin was in France, asking for help. Would John go there and work with him?

Tears ran down Abigail's face. Must she and the children lose John so soon again? How long would he stay across the ocean? "We'll be robbed of our happiness," she sobbed.

But she agreed John must go. "It's your duty to our country," she said with courage.

6. Lonely Days, Lonely Nights

"John, I want to take the children and go with you to France," Abigail pleaded.

"With all my heart I wish you could," John replied. "But if an English ship captures me, I'll end up in prison. I may lose my head. I shudder to think what might happen to you and our little ones."

Together Abigail and John made the decision. "No, the family won't go."

But when Johnny pleaded to go, they said yes. It would be good for the ten-year-old boy to spend more time with his father. Johnny could attend school in France. Schools at home were still closed.

Abigail packed trunks for John and Johnny. She sent a barrel of apples to their ship. At the last moment she sent a few chickens. "They will lay fresh eggs for you while you travel," she said.

The family parted on a cold day in February. Month after long month Abigail waited for a letter. Some people started to say that the ship had been sunk. Others said that Adams was a prisoner.

On the last day of June, Abigail had a letter from John. After a dangerous voyage he was safe in Paris. He was working for his country. Johnny was in school.

They sailed home the next summer. Abigail kissed and hugged them. She thought, "Our family will live together now. I'm so glad."

French ships and French soldiers were fighting on the side of the Americans. John believed that his work in France was done.

But three months later Congress sent him back again. The Americans were winning important battles with the English now. John must be ready to help write the peace treaty when the war was won.

This time John took nine-year-old Charles as well as Johnny. Abigail thought her heart would break.

Again Abigail was the head of the farm and the head of the household. Pretty Nabby helped her mother. Sometimes Abigail took Nabby and Tommy on visits to her two sisters Mary and Elizabeth.

Abigail was brave when she learned that Johnny had gone to Russia. An American diplomat there needed an assistant who could speak and write French. Johnny was only fourteen but he knew the language well.

Without Johnny, Charles grew very homesick. So his father placed him on a ship ready to sail home to Boston. Unexpectedly the ship stopped in Spain and refused to take the passengers any farther. Abigail lived through anxious months until Charles reached her.

Abigail spent many years alone on the farm while John was on business for the new nation.

In the fall of 1781, Washington won the last big battle of the war. The United States had won its independence! Abigail was a proud American.

Her thoughts flew to John. "When will my dear partner come home?"

A year later John still wasn't home. He was working on the peace treaty. Lonely Abigail wrote to him. "Only think how the words three, four, and five years' absence sound! They sink into my heart with a weight I cannot express."

Two years later John still had not come home.

The peace treaty was completed, but Congress had asked John to stay in France. He would help write other treaties so that the United States could carry on business with European countries.

"It's my duty to help our new nation grow great and powerful," John wrote. "Yet I cannot live here any longer without you. Will you come?"

Abigail's heart knew the answer. "Yes!"

7. Across Old Ocean

"I'm going to cross Old Ocean! I'm going to join my partner!" That joyful thought kept running through Abigail's mind as she made plans.

"Nabby will go with me," Abigail said. Her daughter was now a very beautiful eighteen-year-old. "Charles and Tommy will stay here."

They would live with their Aunt Elizabeth. Her husband was a minister and teacher. He would prepare the boys for Harvard College.

Abigail's ship, the *Active,* sailed for England on a warm June day in 1784. Abigail was seasick the first afternoon.

"I smell dirt and that makes me sicker!" she groaned. When she was on her feet again, she got the captain to say she could clean the ship. She told the sailors to bring mops and brushes and pails of water mixed with vinegar. Under her watchful eyes they scrubbed the ship from top to bottom.

A few weeks later Abigail and Nabby reached London. But their letter, telling when they would arrive, hadn't reached John. They had to wait for him.

One afternoon a handsome young man came to their hotel. At first glance he seemed a stranger. Then Abigail looked at him more closely. "My son!" she cried. He had been a twelve-year-old boy when she saw him last. Now he was seventeen and quite grown up. No one called him Johnny any longer. He was now John Quincy.

John was in Holland, where he had been borrowing money for the United States. He finished his work there and hurried to London.

When he swept Abigail into his arms, all the

ache left her heart. Four happy people traveled to Paris. John had rented a mansion outside the city.

Abigail and Nabby went to dinner parties with Benjamin Franklin and Thomas Jefferson. John worked with these men making treaties. John Quincy was his father's secretary.

"I see plays and operas in Paris and I like them," Abigail wrote to her sisters.

She loved to get letters from Charles and Tommy. Elizabeth wrote, "Your boys are doing well in their studies. And at dancing school the misses all like to have Charles for a partner."

In the spring Congress appointed John to be the first American ambassador to England. John Quincy decided to return home and enter Harvard.

"Some day our country will need you as a leader," Abigail said. "Study hard so you will be ready."

A few days later Abigail was packing for the move to London. John entered the room, laughing. "I hear that seven traveling companions were waiting for John Quincy on the ship."

"Who?" asked Abigail quickly.

"Dogs! General Lafayette sent seven hunting dogs to George Washington. John Quincy is to see that they get good food and fresh water."

Abigail laughed so hard that she couldn't pack anything for a few minutes.

8. The Ambassador's Lady

"King George may not be friendly to you," people warned Abigail and John. "Remember, he didn't like to lose America!"

Abigail thought about that warning now. She was at the palace, waiting to meet the king. John had been presented already in a private meeting.

"Oh, I don't tremble before kings," Abigail told herself.

She and Nabby and 200 other guests stood in a circle around a large room. Abigail looked elegant. She wore a long white gown over a wide hoop.

Abigail saw the king enter. He was short and red-faced. Smiling and bowing, he stopped to talk with each person. He did these same things when he reached Abigail.

But he did something more that came as a big surprise. The king kissed Abigail's left cheek!

A few days later Abigail and John and Nabby moved from their hotel to a large house on Grosvenor Square. Abigail had to hire a butler, cook, coachman, and upstairs and downstairs maids.

"Will Congress send enough money for all these expenses?" Abigail worried. Soon she saw that she could save money by doing her own shopping.

The newspapers poked fun at her: "Farmer's wife, going to market!"

The newspapers poked fun at John: "Penny pincher! He doesn't give the dinner parties an ambassador should give."

The fact was that Congress didn't send enough money. Abigail and John weren't rich. John could have earned a great deal of money as a lawyer. But he had given that up long ago when his country needed him.

"We'll act our part well," Abigail said. They would meet the costs somehow. Notes were sent, inviting all the foreign ambassadors to dinner.

"What shall I feed them?" Abigail asked herself.

Before she made up her mind, a wonderful thing happened. A fishing boat arrived from Boston. The captain gave John a giant codfish caught off New England. Abigail's eyes twinkled. "We'll have American food! The codfish will be perfect, served with a tasty sauce." Her dinner party was a success.

At the end of the first year in England, Nabby was married to handsome Colonel William Smith. He was the secretary in the American Embassy. At the end of another year, Abigail was a happy grandmother. "My charmer," she called Nabby's little boy William.

At the end of the third year, John finished his term as ambassador. Abigail was eager to see her sons. She wanted to go home.

Abigail enjoyed the excitement of living in Europe
and being the ambassador's wife. She sat for this
portrait while abroad.

One day, during their last summer in England, John took Abigail to the seashore. She saw men and women bathing in the ocean. They didn't do that back home.

"I'll try it!" said Abigail. She went into a bathhouse. An attendant helped her pull on socks and a flannel gown and an oilcloth cap. Abigail stepped into the salt water.

"It's delightful!" she told John. "We should have our own bathing beach at Braintree!"

9. The Vice-President's Lady

Abigail and John's three handsome sons welcomed them home.

"My dear boys!" Abigail cried.

John Quincy was now studying law. He had finished Harvard with high honors. Charles and Tommy were still students there.

Home for Abigail and John was no longer the small farmhouse. They had bought a large house in nearby Quincy.

Abigail was busy arranging the furniture in their new home. John bought cows. After that he bought sheep and pigs and oxen.

"Your father turned into Farmer John fast!" Abigail wrote to her daughter. Nabby and her family were living near New York City.

In the spring of 1788, John was elected the first vice-president of the United States. It was a great honor. George Washington was elected the first president. The capital was then New York City. Abigail couldn't go there with John when the new government started.

"I must do something with all the animals!" she said. She sold as many as she could. She found someone to take care of the others.

On a June day Abigail reached the comfortable house John had rented in New York. The next morning she visited Martha Washington. The two ladies became warm friends.

Abigail gave pleasant dinner parties for the members of Congress and their wives. She also held open house one evening a week. Everyone was welcome.

John talked with Abigail about the things the new government was planning. She listened carefully. Often she told him what she thought.

"No one is more interested in political subjects than I," Abigail wrote to her sister Elizabeth.

The next year the government was moved to Philadelphia. During her second year there, Abigail had a long, serious illness. When she could stand the bumpy ride in the carriage, John took her home. She got back her health. But she didn't try to live in Philadelphia again while John was vice-president. Each year when Congress finished work, John hurried home to Abigail.

One spring day Abigail received a message that made her proud. President Washington had appointed John Quincy to the position of minister to Holland. He was only twenty-six years old. Yet he was already an ambassador, as his father had been. Tommy would be John Quincy's secretary.

"It's one of my chief blessings to have sons worthy of the trust of our country," Abigail wrote to her two boys. "Serve it with honor as your father does."

10. First Lady

"I'll be with my partner tonight," Abigail told herself as her carriage rattled along.

It was a May morning in 1797. John was now the second president of the United States. Abigail hadn't been with him when he took office in March. She was looking after his sick mother, who was at the end of her long life. After the funeral Abigail left for Philadelphia.

Suddenly Abigail's carriage jerked to a stop. Abigail saw that another carriage had drawn close. A gentleman stepped quickly out.

"John!" cried Abigail.

"I had to come meet you," John said. "I can't

get along without you one more day!" Abigail finished her journey in the president's carriage and at the president's side.

A few days later the new First Lady held a reception. After that she began to give official dinner parties. She also spent much time calling on the ladies who visited her.

"I must return each visit," Abigail wrote to her sister Mary. "I get up at five o'clock in the morning. That's the only way I can do all my work."

Abigail also paid attention to everything that happened in the government. "Politics are as natural to me as breathing," she once remarked. So it was natural that John talked with her about the quarrel between the United States and France.

The quarrel grew until soon the two nations were on the brink of war. Many Americans wanted to fight. They belonged to the party that had voted for John. They were angry when John sent men to France to make peace.

"I know I will not be elected president a second time," John told Abigail.

"You did the right thing," Abigail answered him. Years later all Americans agreed. The young country was saved from a war that would have hurt it.

During John's third year as president, Tommy was back with his parents. Abigail was delighted. Tommy opened a law office in Philadelphia. John

Quincy was now minister to Prussia, which was a part of Germany.

When Congress finished work that spring, Abigail started home ahead of John. On her way she stopped in New York City to see Charles. She did so with a heart heavy with sorrow over this beloved son.

Charles was a lawyer. He had a wife whom Abigail liked and two pretty little girls. But other things hadn't gone well for Charles. When he lost money John Quincy had placed in his care, it was more than Charles could bear. He was drinking heavily. At the age of twenty-nine, Charles was a sick and broken man.

Alone in her room, Abigail wept. She thought back through the years. She could almost hear the little boy say, "I want papa to come home. Take my dollar and get a horse for papa."

Six months later Charles died.

11. The President's House

"We're lost!" said Abigail.

The road was nothing more than two tracks through a thick forest. Abigail's coachman walked ahead and broke off branches so the carriage could squeeze past the trees. Finally a woodcutter directed them to the road for Washington.

When Abigail went to Washington, it was a small town nestled in the lush Virginia countryside.

It was November 1800. Abigail was on her way to join John in the new capital. Four-year-old Susan, Charles's older daughter, was with her.

When she reached the city, Abigail saw the houses were set far apart. Ugly stumps were left where trees had been chopped down. "This is still a wilderness city," she thought.

Abigail caught her first glimpse of the new President's House, later called the White House. It looked twice as big as her church at home. "This house is built for the ages to come," she wrote in a letter to her sister Mary.

Abigail found that not a single room in the

President's House was finished completely. There was also no place outdoors to dry the washing. So she told the servants to hang the laundry in a long parlor, later called the East Room.

She also told the servants, "Please keep all the fires going." The rooms felt cold and damp.

John was delighted to have Abigail and Susan with him. Soon, however, the little girl became sick. Abigail was awakened by dreadful sounds from Susan's room. She was gasping for breath.

"Get a doctor!" cried Abigail. A servant ran for one who lived nearby. The doctor boiled vinegar in a kettle. He had Susan breathe in the steam. In the morning she was better.

In December the votes for president were counted. John was not elected for a second term. He would not be president after March 3.

"You have been a nation-builder. You kept the peace," Abigail said loyally. "I hope future presidents do as much for our country as you have."

She lifted her head proudly. "I will do my duty while we are here." She gave dinner parties and receptions in the unfinished President's House. Her guests included members of Congress, judges, and heads of many departments. Abigail invited their wives too.

In the middle of February, Abigail and Susan started home. John would follow in March. As she rode out of Washington, Abigail thought about the future.

"We'll spend the rest of our lives in Quincy, my partner and I. He will have the farm and his books. Our children and grandchildren will visit us." Abigail laughed aloud and gave Susan a hug. "The family will find me in the dairy early in the morning. I'll be skimming the cream from the milk so I can make good butter for all of us."

And that's what happened. Abigail and John enjoyed many more years together in Quincy. They felt great happiness when John Quincy was made secretary of state. "I pride myself on being the mother of such a son," Abigail said.

Abigail was dead when her son John Quincy was elected the sixth president of the United States. John knew how proud she would have been. Tears rolled down his old cheeks as he thought about her.

"*Dear partner* of all my joys and sorrows. . . ."

DOLLY MADISON
1768-1849

Brave Dolly Madison escaped from the
President's House in 1814 just hours
before the British set fire to it. The little Quaker girl who grew up to be the
First Lady carried to safety the president's papers and the family silver.
She also saved the full-length painting
of George Washington that hangs in
the White House today. When peace
came, the Madisons returned to the
capital city. There lively Dolly was
once more the well-loved hostess of official Washington. At the end of his
second term, James Madison retired.
He and Dolly returned to their home,
Montpelier, in Virginia. Dolly helped
the former president with his work for
20 more years. But she never forgot—
and finally returned to—the city that
had taken her to its heart so long ago.

Dolly Madison
Famous First Lady

by Mary R. Davidson

1. The Little Quaker Girl

A nine-year-old girl hurried along the path to school. Flowers bloomed all around her. Magnolia trees waved their white petals. Virginia was at its loveliest.

The girl was Dolly Payne. She wore a simple gray dress that came down to her ankles. Around her neck was a white kerchief. Under this, on a string, hung her one treasure. It was a little gold pin that her grandmother had given her.

Dolly walked quickly into the schoolroom. She took off her sunbonnet and gloves. She felt under her kerchief to be sure that her pin was safe. She felt again. She couldn't find it!

"Dolly," the Quaker teacher said, "thee is late. Take thy seat."

Dolly sat down. But her mind was on her pin. How could she have lost it! Somehow she got through school that day. She started home, looking carefully on both sides of the road. There was no pin.

She burst into the house, crying, "Mother Amy! Oh, Mother Amy!"

Mother Amy, her black nurse, came hurrying. Dolly threw herself into her arms. "I've lost my pin," she sobbed. "I've looked everywhere."

Mother Amy held her tight. "Your grandma will give you another," she said.

"If she did, I couldn't wear it, because we're Quakers," Dolly sobbed.

Mother Amy spoke more firmly. "Some day, I tell you, you will have lots of gold pins and necklaces. You'll have silk dresses, and velvet ones too."

Dolly looked up, her blue eyes bright with tears. "Do you really think so, Mother Amy?"

"I really do. You just wait, honey."

Dolly (sometimes spelled *Dolley*) was born in North Carolina in 1768. Soon afterward, her parents moved to Virginia.

The Paynes had two sons, Walter and William Temple, who were older than Dolly. There were five younger children: Isaac, Lucy, Mary, Anna, and Johnny. Dolly and Lucy were always close friends. And Dolly loved little Anna dearly.

Dolly's parents were both Quakers. Like most Quakers, Mr. Payne hated fighting. During the Revolutionary War he stayed quietly on his farm, working his fields and feeding his cattle. He did not believe in slavery, for he felt that all men were brothers. He wanted to free the slaves who helped him on his farm, but the laws of Virginia would not allow him to. Mr. Payne helped the poor and cared for the sick. He dressed always in simple clothing.

Dolly's father had not been a Quaker all his life. He had become one when he married Dolly's mother. It was his mother, Mrs. Payne, who had given Dolly the little gold pin.

When Dolly was seven, the Paynes moved to Scotchtown. It was a larger plantation. They had a big house with nineteen rooms. Green fields were all around. A brook, where the children fished, ran through the fields. Every day the children rode horseback, jumping the brook and the stone walls.

The older children attended the nearby Quaker school. There they learned reading, writing, and some arithmetic. Dolly wrote beautifully, but she spelled as she pleased. She spelled *uncle*, "unkle" and *writing*, "wrighting."

Dolly learned as much at home as she did at school. Mrs. Payne was an excellent cook and a woman of great energy and charm. She taught Dolly how to sew, cook, and nurse the sick.

When Dolly was twelve, she made a "trifle." She baked three layers of sponge cake in the brick oven. While these were still hot, she brushed them with rum. Then she spread raspberry jam between the layers and sprinkled sugar on top.

At supper that night, Mr. Payne said, "Mother, this is the best trifle you ever made."

"Your eldest daughter made it," she said. "She'll be a fine cook someday."

After supper the whole family gathered in the living, or "keeping," room. There, standing before the open fire, Mr. Payne read stories to them from the Old Testament. The children listened eagerly.

After this they said good-night. Each one took a candle and went up to bed.

2. Philadelphia

One day when Dolly was fourteen, Mr. Payne called the family and servants together.

"Children," he said, "we are going to move."

There was silence.

Mr. Payne went on. "Virginia has changed the law about freeing slaves, so at last I can free ours. But I will not be able to run the farm without them. We are moving to Philadelphia, where I will go into business."

"Don't free me, Mr. Payne," said Mother Amy. "I want to stay and take care of my children."

Mr. Payne smiled. "I'll have to free you, Mother Amy," he said. "But you may stay with us. I'll pay you wages."

It took a year to free the slaves and sell the

A Philadelphia Quaker family strolls to church on a Sunday morning.

plantation. At last the Paynes packed up their baggage and started for Philadelphia.

Philadelphia was the largest city in the nation. After the quiet of Scotchtown, it seemed crowded and noisy.

But the Paynes' house seemed very small. Mr. Payne needed the big room downstairs for his new business of starch-making. Upstairs there were only six rooms. Dolly had to share a bedroom with her three sisters.

The younger children went to school. Dolly's school days were over, but she had classes in religion. These, her father felt, were important.

In the morning Dolly helped her mother cook. In the afternoon she took long walks with Sally Drinker, her Quaker friend. Their favorite walk took them through the shopping district. Here the stores were filled with beautiful gowns and hats. Some had come straight from Paris. Dolly and Sally both wore plain Quaker dresses, but how they longed for beautiful clothes! One day some new styles were shown.

"Oh, Dolly," Sally cried, "look at that yellow velvet gown! I'd like to have a dress like that!"

They looked in the next store window.

"Look at those little French dolls!" Dolly cried. "They're adorable! Oh, Sally, let's come here often!"

Dolly had a chance to meet other people too. When she was eighteen, she was invited to visit Quaker friends who had a tavern on the King's Highway. Great coaches drawn by four horses stopped there, on their way to New York. Dolly often ran out to greet the passengers. And so she came to know many people who were not Quakers.

The following year the Constitutional Convention was held in Philadelphia. Famous statesmen from all over the country were there, planning the new government. At any time Dolly might see George Washington or Benjamin Franklin walking down the street.

3. Marriage to John Todd

In Philadelphia Dolly was invited to all the parties for young Quakers. No dancing or card playing was allowed. Instead the guests played charades or forfeits.

Many young men admired Dolly. But one young man usually took her home from parties and Quaker meetings. His name was John Todd. John was a young law student. He spent more and more time with Dolly and came to love her.

One night, after John had known Dolly three years, he stopped with her outside her door. He was silent a moment. Then he said, "Dolly, you and I have been together often. You must know that I love you. Will you marry me?"

Dolly hesitated.

John pleaded, "We are both Quakers, and we have the same friends. I think I can make you happy."

Still, Dolly was silent. Then she said, "Oh, John, I don't want to be married yet, not to anyone. Perhaps someday...."

"Then I'll wait," said John. "But I'll always be here to help you and your family. And I'll continue to hope that someday you will say yes."

He bowed and left.

Afterward Dolly kept thinking about John. She *did* like him. But in her heart she hoped sometime to get away from the narrowness of Quaker life. She wanted to meet all kinds of people, to be like other girls.

Meanwhile her father was steadily losing money. Mr. Payne had been a good farmer, but he was a poor businessman. Finally the time came when he could not pay his bills. This made him so discouraged and unhappy that he became sick.

One night he called Dolly to his room. She went to his bedside and gently took his hand.

"Daughter," he said feebly, "has John Todd asked you to marry him?"

Dolly nodded. "Yes, father. He has," she replied. "Do you like him?"

"Oh, yes, father."

"Dolly, John would always love and take care of you." He paused. "I want you to marry him."

Dolly had always obeyed her father. Now as she looked at him, lying weak and sick, her heart went out to him.

"I will, father," she said. "I'll tell John tonight."

A short time afterward, Dolly Payne and John Todd were married at the Quaker meetinghouse. They promised "in the presence of God and of these witnesses" to love each other and to "be faithful unto death."

Eighty people had been invited to the wedding. Afterward they all went to the Paynes' house for a wedding supper.

John was now a successful lawyer. He bought Dolly a house on Chestnut Street in Philadelphia. Later he bought a larger house with a stable and a carriage. For the first time in her life, Dolly could have beautiful things. She bought fine mahogany furniture, curtains, silver, and glass. She loved to keep her house shining and bright.

After two years Dolly and John had a little son. They named him Payne, for Dolly's father.

Dolly was truly happy now. She had a lovely home, a baby boy, and a loving husband.

4. The Yellow Fever

Soon after Dolly's son was born, Mr. Payne died. Dolly's mother had to find a way to support herself.

Philadelphia was now the capital of the United States. There were many congressmen looking for places to take meals. As Mrs. Payne was famous for her cooking, she started a boardinghouse. The young congressmen liked her home-cooked food better than the meals at The Indian Queen, Philadelphia's one hotel.

Lucy, Mary, and Anna lived with their mother and helped her run the boardinghouse.

Dolly came to see her mother often. She enjoyed meeting the congressmen and talking about the government. Aaron Burr, a senator from New York, became a special friend.

One day there was great excitement at Mrs. Payne's boardinghouse. Lucy Payne, fifteen years old, had suddenly eloped with George Steptoe Washington, the president's nephew. Lucy went to live at Harewood, George's home in Virginia. Later Lucy invited her mother and her sister Mary to live with her.

The Paynes were disappointed that Lucy had not married a Quaker. But the marriage proved to be a happy one.

Dolly and John now had another baby, a boy named William. They were happier than ever. But suddenly a dreadful sickness called yellow fever swept Philadelphia.

No one was safe. The fever victims suffered terribly. They died in a few hours. The doctors didn't know what to do. They drew blood from people. They fired cannons, hoping to clear the air of fever. Nothing could stop the epidemic. Everyone tried to get out of the city.

John Todd took Dolly and the children to a safe place in the country. Then he hurried back to Philadelphia.

John gave money to help the sufferers. And like a good Quaker, he himself took care of the sick and dying.

Then his parents, who were still in the city, came down with the yellow fever. John wrote Dolly that he was looking after them.

Dolly was terribly worried. She knew John was very tired. She was afraid he would be sick himself.

In spite of everything John did, his parents died. He attended to the burial. Then, on horseback, he started for the country and Dolly.

As he was riding, he began to have dreadful pain. He knew what that meant, for he had taken care of many people with the yellow fever. His one thought was to see Dolly again. As he rode, he kept saying over and over again, "I must see her! I must see her! I must see her!"

So he kept on going. He did reach Dolly. She ran out to meet him. She knew he was sick, but she was not afraid. She threw her arms around him. She helped him from his horse.

"John, dear," she whispered.

But John could not answer her. He died almost immediately.

The very next day, Dolly herself was sick. Her mother came at once to nurse her. Dolly fought her way through the fever. She began to get well. Bravely, she tried to face the idea of life without John.

Then one morning Mrs. Payne came into Dolly's room. Her face was very sad.

"Dolly," she began, "the baby . . ."

"Not the yellow fever!" Dolly cried. "Oh, no, mother, not the yellow fever."

Mrs. Payne nodded. "I'm afraid it is," she said softly.

"Please bring him to me, mother."

Mrs. Payne brought in the three-month-old baby. Dolly looked at him. She knew that nothing could be done. The little boy lived only a few hours. Dolly held him to the end.

These were the saddest days of Dolly's life.

5. Mrs. James Madison

When Dolly returned to Philadelphia, her sister Anna came to live with her. Dolly got well surprisingly fast. As she grew stronger, she became prettier than ever. People turned to look at her on the street.

Her friend, Aaron Burr, came to call often. One day Burr said to Dolly, "James Madison would like very much to meet you. May I bring him over some afternoon?"

Dolly said, "Of course!"

Madison was a congressman from Virginia. He was a famous man who had done much of the planning of the Constitution. And then, with Alexander Hamilton and John Jay, he had written the *Federalist Papers*. These papers were written to get people to approve the Constitution. Madison had kept a written record of the debates at the Constitutional Convention. This record was valuable because it was the only one.

Now Madison was working on the famous amendments to the Constitution which were later called the Bill of Rights.

Madison was brilliant and wealthy, but he was rather quiet and shy. He was seventeen years older than Dolly.

Burr took him to see Dolly as planned. They

found her in a room lighted by many candles. She wore a dark red satin dress with a fine white kerchief. A little lace cap was on her dark curls. Madison had never seen anyone so lovely. That afternoon he fell in love with her.

Madison wanted to be married at once, but Dolly hesitated. She wanted to have time to think things over, so she went to visit Lucy in Virginia. On the way she stopped at an inn. Suddenly she knew she wanted to marry Madison.

James Madison

Madison hurried to Harewood, Lucy's home. He and Dolly were married there.

Dolly's first wedding had been a quiet one. But this wedding was very gay. There was dancing. Violins and banjos played minuets and lively reels.

"Ladies change! Grand right and left!" the caller shouted.

Dolly wore a beautiful wedding gown. Madison wore a silk coat, and he had diamond buckles on his shoes. Ladies cut off pieces from his ruffled shirt to keep as souvenirs.

Finally Dolly and Madison got away in a shower of rice and flowers.

Madison had wanted to take Dolly to Montpelier, his home in Virginia. But there was no time for a honeymoon. He was needed in Philadelphia.

Madison was not a Quaker, and Dolly herself was no longer a Quaker. She now wore the gay dresses and jewelry that she had longed for as a girl. But she never forgot the Quaker lessons of duty and kindness.

Her first thought was always for her husband. As Madison was not strong, it was necessary to guard his health.

Payne, too, was always on her mind. But she was not wise with him. She let him do anything he wanted. Madison, who loved Payne as if he were his own son, also spoiled him.

Dolly enjoyed being with her two sisters. Anna still lived with her. Mary was invited up from Harewood. The three sisters went to parties and balls. Dolly wanted them to have all the fun that she herself had missed as a girl.

Dolly had never learned to dance. But Anna and Mary had learned how. They had many a gay time with their older sister as chaperone.

6. The Nation's Hostess

When Dolly married Madison, there were two political parties in America. There were the Federalists and the Democrats. The Federalists believed that the rich landowners and businessmen should run the country. The Democrats thought that the common people should have more power. In 1794 John Adams, a Federalist, became president. Madison, a Democrat, left Congress and went home to Montpelier.

Madison's estate was at its loveliest. The brick house stood high on a hill facing the Blue Ridge Mountains. Someone said that Montpelier was only "a squirrel's throw from heaven."

Dolly loved Montpelier. She loved the flowering trees, the redbud and the dogwood.

Shortly after his marriage, James added a portico and wings to the square house. His mother and father moved into the south wing.

Madison kept in close touch with politics. He and Jefferson, then vice-president, wrote to each other often.

In 1801 Jefferson himself was elected president. The first thing he did was to make James Madison his secretary of state.

The Madisons moved to Washington, which was now the nation's capital. Dolly had many visitors. Jefferson noticed how nicely Dolly entertained. Mr. Jefferson's own wife had died, and his two daughters were both married. So he asked Dolly to be the nation's official hostess.

During Jefferson's administration, the spirit of adventure and progress swept the nation. The United States purchased the Louisiana Territory from France. Madison had worked hard for this.

The news reached Washington early on the morning of July 3, 1803.

Madison was awakened by the ringing of bells and the roaring of cannons.

A messenger burst in, shouting, "The United States has bought Louisiana!"

Madison hurried to the President's House to help prepare a statement. The next day there was a grand celebration. Dolly rounded up her many helpers. Together they prepared cakes and drinks. These were served to hundreds of hungry people who crowded the streets. Everyone was happy and excited.

The same eager spirit of progress was shown in an expedition to the Northwest. This was led by Captain Meriwether Lewis, Jefferson's secretary, and his friend, Captain William Clark. For years Jefferson had wanted to map the territory between the Mississippi River and the Pacific Ocean. Now, after careful preparation, Lewis and Clark set out. Before the men left, Dolly gave a dinner in their honor.

A great tragedy occurred the following year. The vice-president of the United States killed one of the nation's greatest statesmen—Aaron Burr shot Alexander Hamilton in a duel. Burr had been angered by something Hamilton had said about him. Everyone was shocked. Hamilton had been the nation's first secretary of the treasury. Dolly must have been horrified, because Burr had been her friend.

There was happiness for Dolly, however, as well as sadness, for Dolly's sister Anna had recently married Richard Cutts. He was a congressman from Massachusetts. Because their husbands were both in the government, the two sisters saw each other often.

7. First Lady of the Land

In 1809 James Madison was inaugurated president of the United States. Dolly Madison was the new First Lady of the Land.

Jefferson was glad to have his friend take his place. Now Dolly was truly the nation's official hostess.

Inauguration Day began with a long parade in honor of Madison. That night there was a gay Inaugural Ball. This was the first Inaugural Ball in the nation's history. It took place in a large hall in a hotel. The room was so crowded that windows had to be broken to let in air. Dolly was lovely in a yellow velvet dress. There were pearls at her neck and wrists. On her head was a turban from Paris with two beautiful plumes.

At first the Madisons had to live in their own home. Jefferson had brought his furniture and belongings to the empty President's House. Now he carted all his things back to his home, Monticello, in Virginia.

"I believe the President's House belongs to the people," Dolly said. "It should be beautiful and have things of its own."

Congress agreed and gave money for furniture. Dolly and an architect started picking things out.

Dolly decided to use many mirrors. "These will

Dolly was such a popular First Lady that people everywhere copied her clothes. She was known for her beautiful turbans.

make the rooms seem larger and reflect the lights of the crystal chandeliers."

She had chairs, sofas, and hangings of yellow satin damask. Stuart's famous painting of George Washington was hung in the dining room. Dolly bought a piano, a guitar, and a parrot.

Dolly was now so popular that people copied everything she did. They copied her clothes. They copied her dinners. They copied what she said. Dolly was so interested in all people that she remembered not only the faces but also the names of everyone she met.

Dolly's dinners were famous. The table was piled with delicious foods of all kinds. Her ice cream, which was a new treat then, proved to be very popular.

Dolly and Madison had no children other than Payne. But Dolly tried to make other people's children happy. She started Easter egg rolling on the front lawn of the Capitol building. She also helped to start an orphanage. She herself made clothes for the orphans.

Dolly's son, Payne, was a young man now. Dolly gave parties for his friends. She took them to the races. She sent Payne abroad. He never wrote home. He borrowed money from Madison but never returned it. Dolly could not stop loving Payne. But he made her very unhappy.

8. Washington Burns

Ever since the Revolutionary War, America had had trouble with England. In 1812 war began again. At first the fighting was at sea and on the Great Lakes. Then in 1814 the British landed at the mouth of the Potomac River. They were marching toward Washington, bent on burning the city.

Madison told Dolly, "My place, as commander in chief, is with the army. Would you be afraid to stay here with a guard?"

"No," said Dolly, firmly.

"Good. Save everything you can, especially my government papers. Pack them in trunks and send them to a safe place. I'll send word where I can meet you. Take care of yourself."

Soon after Madison left, Dolly went up to the housetop. Through her spyglass she could faintly make out a moving line of men. She could hear the roar of distant cannons.

"John," she called to her faithful servant. "Come and help me pack Mr. Madison's papers."

The sound of cannons came nearer. Someone shouted, "The guard has fled!" But Dolly kept on working. She packed the silver and other valuables in big baskets ready to take away with her.

The next morning Dolly was calmly writing to

her sister when a soldier dashed up. He brought a note from Madison.

"Leave at once," it said. "You are no longer safe."

Dolly started to leave. Then she thought of Stuart's portrait of Washington.

"We must save the painting of President Washington!" she called.

John found the frame was nailed to the wall.

"Break the frame," commanded Dolly.

John broke the frame. The picture was given to two men, who carried it safely to New York.

Then Dolly and Sukey hurried away in a carriage. They took the silver and other valuables with them.

The Capitol building was set on fire by the advancing British troops in the War of 1812.

Roads out of the city were jammed with carts and people trying to escape.

The British came up steadily. They entered Washington. Shouting wildly, they set fire to the Capitol building. Then they burned down the Library of Congress with all its valuable books.

Next, they went to the President's House. Hundreds of soldiers roamed through the rooms. They piled Dolly's beautiful furniture and Madison's books in the center of the rooms. They threw flaming balls of paper through the windows. Soon the furniture and books caught on fire. The heat was so great that it melted some statues and glass chandeliers.

Meanwhile, Dolly and Sukey rushed through Georgetown at top speed. They spent the first night at a military camp. The next day Dolly drove to the place where she had arranged to meet Madison. He was there, and they talked. But a report came that he was in danger. So he and his guards fled into the woods for safety.

Now Dolly was on her own. She sent Sukey away in the carriage with the silver. Then she dressed like a poor country woman and started off in a farm wagon. Two men went with her.

For two days Dolly drove through the country. People feared she was lost.

Meanwhile a terrible hurricane hit Washington. It

ripped the roofs off houses and tipped over the British cannons. For hours the rain fell in torrents, putting out the fires. The British became tired and discouraged. They were happy when orders came to leave the ruined city.

Dolly found her way to the Potomac River. The bridge to Washington was down at both ends. Dolly saw an officer in a ferryboat. She asked him to take her across. He looked at her ragged clothes and refused.

"I am the president's wife," she said.

The officer laughed, "You really don't expect me to believe that!"

Finally she convinced him. He took her across the river to Washington. She found only rubble and smoldering ashes where once great buildings had stood.

Dolly drove at once to see her sister, Anna Cutts. Anna's house was still standing. Here Madison joined Dolly. At last they were together and safe.

9. Rebuilding the Capital

General Andrew Jackson won a great victory over the British at New Orleans in 1815. Very soon afterward came wonderful news. A treaty had been signed with England. The people went wild.

Bells rang. Fireworks lighted the sky. Bonfires blazed from Boston to Washington.

The Madisons were living in a mansion called Octagon House. Crowds of people filled the drawing room. Dolly, happy and relaxed, looked her loveliest.

Now the first job was to rebuild Washington. The architect Benjamin Henry Latrobe was called in. He had helped plan the capital earlier. Now he cut down trees along Pennsylvania Avenue to make room for new buildings.

The Capitol itself consisted of two great buildings with a muddy walk between. Charles Bulfinch of Boston put in a central building, connecting the two already there. Bulfinch planned a dome to go above the central part.

The Library of Congress with all its priceless books was gone. In order to start the new library, Thomas Jefferson sent his own books. There were several thousand of them. Ten yoke of oxen pulled the precious books from Monticello to Washington.

The inside of the President's House was entirely burned out. But the outer walls remained. These, black with smoke, were now painted white. The Madisons lived in a house on Pennsylvania Avenue while this work was being done. When the work was finished, they moved back into the President's House.

Because it was painted white, the President's House was soon being called the White House. This name has lasted through the years.

Dolly still gave her delightful parties. She still found time to help the orphans. And every day boys and girls gathered outside the window where her famous parrot sat in the sunshine.

By the end of his second term, Madison was 66 years old. He had been president of the United States for eight years. He had led the nation through a war. He had seen Washington burned to the ground, then rebuilt through his tireless efforts. He had been unpopular at first because many people disliked the idea of war. But he was much loved by the end of his presidency.

Now Madison was ready to retire from politics. Dolly, although seventeen years younger, was also tired of political life. They were both glad to leave the presidency to their good friend James Monroe. They longed to go home to Montpelier.

10. Montpelier

Montpelier was larger than ever. It covered between three and four thousand acres. There were fields of tobacco and grain, and meadows for the grazing cattle. The house itself was large, and the rooms were bright and airy.

Montpelier, the beautiful home of Dolly and James

Madison's father had died. But Madison's mother still lived in her wing of the house. She and Dolly became close friends. Dolly took all her famous guests to call on the old lady.

The most important room in the house was the library. But it was so jammed with books and papers that Madison worked in his sitting room. He was completing his record of the Constitutional Convention. Dolly helped him copy his papers.

Many guests came to Montpelier. Dolly never knew how many would be there for meals, or to spend the night. One day there were 90 people at an outdoor dinner. But there was plenty of food, and room to spare.

One very important guest was General Lafayette. He was the famous French general who had helped America win the Revolutionary War.

Lafayette landed in New York, where he was given a great public welcome. He visited Jefferson, who was now a very old man. Then Lafayette with his son, friends, secretary, and servants came to Montpelier.

"They're coming! They're coming!" called a little boy.

Up the long drive wound a long procession of coaches and men on horseback. They drew near the house. There on the porch, the Madison family was gathered.

"Welcome, General Lafayette!" they shouted. "Welcome!"

Lafayette stayed for several weeks with the Madisons. He was interested in Dolly's garden. Later he sent her lilies from France. He sat with Madison by the fire. They talked about the affairs of the United States and France.

All this entertaining was delightful, but expensive. Madison had to sell some of his land to pay his bills. But guests kept coming.

Meanwhile Payne was in Europe, having a gay time. He sent home for so much money that Madison had to cut off his allowance. Then no word came for months. Finally, they learned that

Payne was in prison for not paying his debts. Money was sent at once, and Payne came home.

The years passed. Each year found Dolly a little older, a little more tired. Each year Madison suffered more and more from rheumatism. After a while he had to be taken around in a wheelchair. But he was always cheerful, never complaining.

Dolly never left his side. For twenty years this gay, lively woman stayed at Montpelier. She used all her ability and charm to keep her beloved husband happy.

Suddenly Madison grew much weaker. On June 28, 1836, he died. He had been so quiet and brave that no one realized how sick he really was.

With Madison's death the nation lost the "Father of the Constitution" and one of its most devoted and brilliant statesmen.

11. Dolly's Last Years

In his will Madison left Montpelier to Dolly. She decided to put her son in charge of the farm. Dolly hoped he would really get to work at last. She left Payne alone and returned to Washington. She was now 69.

Dolly owned a small house in the center of the city. Anna Payne, her brother's daughter, lived there with her.

Soon Dolly started entertaining again. Her old friends came to see her often. She gave several parties. One was a gay wedding reception when her nephew, Richard Cutts, married the grand-daughter of Thomas Jefferson.

Usually, at these parties, Dolly wore the same black velvet gown. She had very little money now, and her other dresses were shabby. But her charm and dignity had not changed.

At Montpelier Payne could not earn a living. Because he had never worked, he did not know how to run a farm.

Dolly's rides through the streets of Washington took her past the restored White House.

To help him, Dolly mortgaged her Washington house. Finally she had to sell beautiful Montpelier with its gardens and great trees. She kept only the family burial ground and a little furniture. Later she sold her valuable Stuart paintings and some silver. Now Dolly was very poor.

Sometimes Dolly would have gone hungry had it not been for the Daniel Websters. They lived across the street from her and sent her food.

On Dolly's 80th birthday a wonderful thing happened. Congress bought her husband's records of the Constitutional Convention for $25,000. Dolly had been trying to sell the papers for years. They were put in the Library of Congress. They are still kept there.

The money came at the time of Dolly's greatest need. It changed everything. Her fear of poverty was gone.

Congress gave Dolly a seat in the House of Representatives. From here, she could watch everything going on. Never before had a seat in the House been given to any woman.

Dolly was an old lady now. But she still invited to every big public event. Samuel F. B. Morse, the inventor, asked her to be one of a small group present when his first telegram was sent. It was sent from Baltimore, Maryland, to Washington.

Dolly, at 78, still glowed with a love of life.

"What hath God wrought" was the message that came over the telegraph wire.

Mr. Morse turned to Dolly. "Mrs. Madison, would you send a return message?"

Dolly thought a moment. Then she sent greetings to an old friend in Baltimore.

Dolly was also present when the cornerstone of the Washington Monument was laid. She, who had known and loved Washington, rode in the parade to honor him.

Dolly's last public appearance was at President

James Polk's farewell ball. The White House was brilliantly lighted and crowded with people. Toward the end of the ball, the president asked Dolly to walk about with him. Dolly was dressed in a white satin gown and white satin turban. Slowly she went through the rooms on the president's arm. The people all greeted her with deep affection.

The summer of 1849 was very hot. Dolly did not complain, but she felt ill. She went to bed and was content to stay there. One night she fell quietly asleep. In the morning she did not awaken.

All Washington turned out at Dolly's funeral. The president and members of the Cabinet were there. Senators and members of the House of Representatives marched in the funeral procession. There were officers of the army and navy, ambassadors from foreign countries, and members of the Supreme Court.

Dolly had touched the lives of thousands of people and had left them all happier for having known her. The secret of her popularity may be found in a conversation she had with a visiting Frenchman.

"Everyone loves Mrs. Madison," he said, smiling down at her.

Dolly answered quickly, "Mrs. Madison loves everybody."

MARY TODD LINCOLN
1818-1882

From the moment they met, Mary Todd
knew that the tall, ungainly-looking Mr.
Lincoln would go far. In time, she married the young backwoods lawyer. Mary
encouraged Abe to run for Congress
and later for the presidency. His election to the highest office in the land
was a dream come true. All too soon
the Civil War began. The terrible fighting cast a shadow on their lives. The
death of their small son Willie filled
them with sadness. And public disap-
proval of Mary became almost too
much for her to bear. Peace finally
came to the divided country and with
it the promise of happier times. The
promise soon turned to tragedy when
Abraham Lincoln was killed by an
assassin's bullet. Mary Todd Lincoln
had, in a few short years, tasted the
greatest of joys—and enough sorrow to
last several lifetimes.

Mary Todd Lincoln
President's Wife

by LaVere Anderson

1. Girl of Kentucky

"Lizzie, come look out the window! Hurry!" Mary Todd cried. "There is a man hiding by the back fence."

Her cousin ran to the window. "It's almost too dark to see—," she began. "Oh, you mean that dark shadow under the willow tree! Do you suppose he is a robber?"

The two girls were in Mary's bedroom in the beautiful Todd home in Lexington, Kentucky. It was a summer evening in 1829. Mary had been born in Lexington on December 13, 1818. Cousin Lizzie Humphreys was visiting the Todds and shared Mary's room.

"Look, there's Mammy Sally going out to him," Mary said. "She's carrying something in a sack."

Lizzie leaned out the open window to see better. "She's giving the sack to him. Why, she's friends with a robber!"

"She is not!" Mary said. Mammy Sally was the kindly black woman who took care of the Todd children. Mary loved her and trusted her. She knew Mammy Sally would not do anything wrong.

The shadow slipped away into the night. Mammy Sally came back across the yard.

"Let's go ask her who the man was," Mary said. She led the way down the stairs to the big kitchen. Mammy Sally was alone. She looked worried when the girls told her what they had seen.

"Was that a robber?" Lizzie asked.

"He was only a hungry man. I gave him some food," Mammy Sally answered.

"Why didn't he come to the house to eat?" Mary asked. "Ma always feeds anyone who comes. Why was he hiding?"

Mammy Sally looked more worried than ever. At last she said, "Can you girls keep a secret?" The girls nodded.

"He was a runaway slave," Mammy Sally said. "There are a lot of poor black men like him trying to get away from bad slave owners. If they can reach Canada, they will be free and safe. I have put a mark on the fence to show I will feed anyone who needs help. Other slaves pass the word to the runaways. After dark every night I keep watch, and when I see someone I go out."

The girls' eyes grew wide. They knew it was dangerous to help runaways. The slaves' masters could make trouble for anyone who did.

Mary threw her arms around her brave old

nurse. "We'll never tell," she promised. "I am glad you help the men. I will help too if I can. But Canada is a long way off, isn't it?"

"A long, hard way," Mammy Sally said sadly. "Most of them will be caught before they can get there."

The next morning the girls went to look at the back fence. They found a deep cut Mammy Sally had made in the wood. Near the fence stood the willow tree. Mary walked over to it. Suddenly she said, "These long, thin willow branches are soft enough to bend into hoops. Let's pick some and sew them inside our Sunday dresses. I'm tired of little-girl clothes. Hoop skirts are so pretty."

"We are too young for hoop skirts," Lizzie said. "What will Aunt Betsy say?"

"When she sees how pretty our dresses are—," Mary began. Then she stopped. What *would* her stepmother, Betsy, say? "Ma is always wanting me to be a lady. And hoop skirts are *very* ladylike!"

Mary began to break branches from the tree. Soon Lizzie was helping her. When they had gathered enough, they hurried to their room.

"I'm glad Elizabeth did not see us," Mary said. "She would have asked all sorts of questions."

Elizabeth was Mary's oldest sister. Mary had two other sisters and two brothers. They were the children of Robert Smith Todd and his first wife.

Mary's mother had died when Mary was six. Later Mr. Todd had married again. Now he and the second Mrs. Todd had small children.

All that Saturday Mary and Lizzie worked away. By evening their little white skirts swelled from the hoops sewn into them.

"We will wear them to Sunday School tomorrow," Mary said happily.

Sunday morning the girls put on their hoop dresses and went proudly down to breakfast. The family was in the dining room.

"My goodness, just look at Mary and Lizzie!" Elizabeth exclaimed. "Ugh, what a sight!"

Everybody stared. Then some of the children laughed.

"Girls!" Mrs. Todd gasped. "What have you done to your dresses?"

"We've put hoops in them, ma," Mary cried. "Aren't they pretty?"

"They are—grotesque!" Mrs. Todd said. "Both of you must change your dresses at once."

Lizzie ran from the room. Mary began to cry.

"You are all just mean!" she shouted between sobs. "It's not fair that I can't have pretty clothes!"

"Mary, dear—," Mrs. Todd said. But Mary was deaf to anybody's words but her own. "I won't change my dress!" she cried. She turned and ran out into the garden. The whole family was mean, she thought, and her stepmother was the worst of all.

"My dress is *not* grotesque," she told herself. She looked down at it. Suddenly she saw how crooked the hoops were, and how the dark wood showed through the thin white cloth. She pulled at her skirt to straighten it. It still hung twisted and out of shape. Why, she had been so busy fixing it that she had never really looked at it!

Mary was a quick-tempered girl, but she was also an honest one. "Ma was right," she said aloud. Shame swept over her. How could she make up to her mother for her rudeness?

Suddenly she spied a perfect red rosebud. "Ma loves roses," she thought. She picked the bud. Head high, she marched back to the dining room. Mary went straight to her mother and handed her the rosebud.

Mrs. Todd understood. "Thank you, my little Mary," she said.

Chaney, the cook, came in with a tray of food. "Everybody eat these hotcakes before they are cold-cakes," she ordered.

Mary looked at her mother. "Shall I change after breakfast, ma?" Lizzie had already changed and was at the table.

Mrs. Todd nodded. She pinned the rosebud to

her dress. A smile lit Mary's face as she sat down. Ma was going to wear the rose to church! No girl in Lexington could cry harder than Mary Todd. But none had a sunnier smile either.

2. Dinner with Henry Clay

"One—two—three—and turn!" In a loud voice Madame Mentelle counted out the steps for her dancing class. "Keep time to the music, girls. One —two—"

Thirteen-year-old Mary stepped and turned. She liked to dance.

"One—two—three—and curtsy!" said Madame Mentelle. "Very good. That is enough dancing for today. It is time now for your French class."

Mary liked to speak French just as much as she liked to dance. She liked to read too, and to write poetry.

"Mary is smart and quick to learn," her teachers said.

It was no secret that Mary Todd was the best student in Madame Mentelle's school for girls in Lexington.

Mary's father was a rich man, and he saw to it that his children were given the finest training. At home Mary always had good books to read. And there was good conversation.

Mary's tall, quiet father was her hero. He was a businessman and had been a state senator. Like his family before him, he was interested in politics. In the Todd family there had been governors, senators, and judges.

Mr. Todd often talked to Mary about politics. He explained how men were elected to run the government. He told her how important it was to elect wise men. Sometimes he took her with him when he visited political friends. In those days most girls were not interested in politics, but Mary was different. She loved the excitement of meeting famous people.

Many important men visited Lexington. Often Mr. Todd invited them to his big brick home for dinner. When they talked about government matters, Mary listened with sharp ears. Sometimes she joined in.

"Old Andrew Jackson is putting on a lively campaign for reelection to the presidency," a visitor said one day. "When he comes to Lexington, there is to be a big picnic for him."

"There are other men who would make better presidents of the United States," Mr. Todd said.

"Mr. Jackson won't be reelected," Mary spoke up suddenly. "He will be snowed under by so many votes for Henry Clay that his long face will freeze. He will never be able to smile again."

The men laughed. But Mrs. Todd shook her head. She did not think it was ladylike to say such things.

Henry Clay was one of Mr. Todd's Lexington friends. He had held many high offices. Mary had known him since she was a baby, and she often visited his beautiful home, Ashland.

"Mr. Henry Clay is the handsomest man in town and has the best manners of anybody—except my father," Mary said.

So when her father gave her a new pony, Mary rode it to Ashland. A servant came to the door. "Mr. and Mrs. Clay have guests," he told her.

"Tell him that Miss Mary Todd is calling," young Mary said grandly.

Soon Mr. Clay came out, a smile on his face.

"I've brought my new pony to dance for you," Mary cried. She raised the reins, and the white pony reared and pawed the air.

Mr. Clay clapped his hands. "What a smart pony!" he said. He lifted Mary from her saddle. "You must join us for dinner."

Seated in the big dining room, Mary almost forgot to eat. She was too busy listening to the men talk about politics. At last she could keep quiet no longer.

"Mr. Clay, my father says you will be the next president of the United States," she said. "I wish I could go to Washington and live in the White House. I begged my father to be president, but he only laughed. He said he would rather see you there than be president himself."

"Well," said Henry Clay, "if I am ever president, I shall expect Mary Todd to be one of my first guests."

Mary's cheeks turned pink with pleasure.

"Someday I shall visit the White House!" she thought.

3. Happy Young People

The years passed quickly for Mary. Almost before she knew it, her school days were over. She had gone to school much longer than most girls of her time. After Madame Mentelle's, she had studied for two years with Dr. John Ward. He was one of the best teachers in Lexington.

When she was 20, Mary visited her sister Elizabeth in Springfield, Illinois. Elizabeth had married Ninian Edwards, son of the governor of Illinois.

Springfield was a small town, but it was the new capital of the state. There were many political meetings and many parties. After the quiet of Lexington, Mary loved the gay, busy life in Springfield.

Abraham Lincoln as a young man

Mary's cousin John Todd Stuart also lived in Springfield. He had a young law partner named Abraham Lincoln.

Mary first met Abraham Lincoln at a party. She looked very pretty that night. Her blue eyes were shining, and she wore a rose in her brown hair.

"Miss Todd, I want to dance with you in the worst way," Abraham Lincoln said.

He did dance with her in the worst way. Awkward Abe stepped all over her slippers!

Abe Lincoln was so tall that Mary came only to his shoulder. He had black hair that would not stay combed and a thin, homely face. But his gray eyes were kind and full of fun. Mary liked him.

After that party Abraham Lincoln often went to the Edwardses' big house to see Mary. The two found they were interested in many of the same things. They read books together and wrote funny poems. They talked about politics. Mary told him of her home in Kentucky.

"I was born in Kentucky too," he said, "in a log cabin. When I was about six, my father put an ax in my hands and set me to work chopping down trees. Everybody had to work hard to get enough to eat. I went to school for only about three months. Anything else I know I learned by myself from books."

People began to make jokes to Mary about her "tall beau." But Mary had many gentlemen friends. One was Stephen A. Douglas, another lawyer.

"Young Douglas is smart," Ninian told Mary and Elizabeth one evening as they sat at supper. "He is going to be an important man someday."

"So is Mr. Lincoln," Mary said.

Elizabeth looked troubled. "Mary, I wish you were not so friendly with Mr. Lincoln. He is different from you. You grew up in a beautiful home and went to the best schools. He grew up in the backwoods among rough people. He does not even know how to dress or how to act at a party. I don't understand what you see in someone like him."

"I see someone kind and good," Mary said. "He has a fine mind, and he has taught himself."

"He will be a poor man all his life," said Ninian.

Mary did not care if Abraham Lincoln was poor. They had good times together. Before long they fell in love.

"I am going to marry Mr. Lincoln," Mary told her sister and brother-in-law.

"Oh, Mary, I can't let you make such a bad mistake," Elizabeth cried.

Mary's eyes flashed angrily. "Do not say one word against him, for I will not listen to you," she told her sister.

Elizabeth and Ninian saw that Mary would not change her mind. So Ninian said, "We will have the wedding here."

It was raining hard in Springfield on the cold, dark night of November 4, 1842. But inside the Edwardses' big house every lamp was lit. Open fires burned brightly. Many of their friends were there to help eat the wedding cake that stood on the dining room table.

Mary looked lovely in a white dress. She was very happy as she and her "tall beau" were married. On her finger Abraham Lincoln placed a gold wedding ring. He had had three words put inside the ring. They were: "Love is eternal."

4. The Congressman's Wife

Mary was busy in the kitchen making apple pies. Two small boys played on the floor with a toy wagon. Out in the backyard Abraham Lincoln chopped stove wood. Soon he came into the kitchen with an armload of sticks.

"Is this enough wood to cook pies?" he asked.

"Plenty," Mary said. "Oh, just think how long it will be before I make pies in this kitchen again!"

He grinned. "Are you already sorry that we are going to Washington, Molly?"

"Of course not, Mr. Lincoln!" Mary said. She called him "Mr. Lincoln," and he called her "Molly." "I am proud that my husband has been elected to Congress. I'll like living in Washington."

Much had happened to Mr. and Mrs. Abraham Lincoln in the five years since they had married. Two sons were born—Bob, now four, and Eddy, who was not yet two. Mr. Lincoln had made such a good name as a lawyer that he had just been elected to the House of Representatives. Soon the family would leave Springfield for the nation's capital.

Several days later the Lincolns started out. They planned to stop on the way for a visit with the Todds in Kentucky. Most of the Todds had never met Abraham Lincoln.

It was a long, hard trip from Springfield to Lexington. It took almost two weeks by stagecoach, by riverboat, and on a noisy little train. In Lexington old Nelson met their train. He was the Todd coachman, and he was wearing his best blue coat with silver buttons.

"My, I'm glad to see you again, Miss Mary!" he said as he led them to the carriage.

In the big Todd house, the Lincolns found the family waiting for them.

"Pa! Ma!" Mary cried. "I have brought my husband and sons to show them off to you." Excitement made Mary's blue eyes shine as the Todds welcomed Abraham Lincoln.

She hugged her young stepbrothers and sisters. There were eight of them now. Emilie was the youngest. The pretty little girl was frightened when she saw so many strangers. The tall man in the black coat frightened her most of all.

"Is he a giant?" she asked.

Abraham Lincoln loved children. He reached down and picked her up. "So this is little sister," he said.

Emilie looked into the giant's friendly face. Suddenly she felt safe in his strong arms. "I'm not afraid of you anymore," she whispered.

Like Emilie, all the Todds were soon good friends with Abraham Lincoln. Mr. and Mrs. Todd invited many people to their home to meet him. Chaney kept the dinner table loaded with chicken and turkey, sweet potatoes, orange cake, and fresh hot bread spread with honey. "No one can cook like Chaney!" Mary said.

One day Mary took her husband to visit her grandmother. Grandmother Parker lived in a large and beautiful house. But nearby, behind a tall fence, stood a row of small ugly buildings that looked like pens. When runaway slaves were caught, they were kept in the pens until their masters came for them.

As the Lincolns sat with Grandmother Parker on her porch, they heard terrible cries coming from the pens. It sounded as though some of the slaves were being whipped.

Abraham Lincoln's face grew sad. He told Mary, "Where I lived, I never saw slaves when I was young. You grew up among them."

"Yes," Mary said. "Lexington is lovely, but there has always been this dark, dreadful side of life here. I used to see slaves sold in the town square. Poor mothers would weep as their children were sold away from them. Pa was against slavery, yet he owned Nelson and Chaney and Mammy Sally. They were slaves, but they were like part of the family too. I used to wonder when I was a child if they *minded* being slaves!"

Grandmother Parker spoke up. "I have planned to free my slaves. Slavery is wrong."

Abraham Lincoln nodded. "It is a wrong that has come to us from the past. No man should own another man."

"I feel that way too," Mary said.

Soon after visiting Grandmother Parker, the Lincolns went to Washington. There they rented rooms in a boardinghouse. Mary often took the children for walks or to play in a nearby park.

Sometimes Congressman Lincoln joined his family for a walk. One day they were passing the White House. With a grin he stopped and pointed at it. "It is too bad that Henry Clay was never elected president. You didn't get to visit the White House."

"Mr. Clay would have been a good president," Mary said, "but you would be a better one."

"Imagine me being president!" her husband laughed. "No one but you would think of such a thing, Molly."

"You wait and see, Mr. Lincoln," his wife said. "Someday a lot of people will think of it."

5. At Home in Springfield

Mary liked the nation's capital. Still, she was glad when it was time to go home. "Washington and Lexington are lovely," Mary said, "but Springfield is the best place of all."

Springfield was still a small town. The sidewalks were made of wooden boards, and pigs rolled in the mud and dust of the streets. The Lincolns had a small story-and-a-half brown house on the corner of Eighth and Jackson streets. Three blocks past their house the farm country began.

They kept a horse and a cow. They got their water from a well in the backyard and wood from a woodpile. Every morning Mary cleaned and filled the oil lamps.

It was a happy home until little Eddy grew sick and died. Losing him nearly broke the Lincolns' hearts. But in time two more sons were born—Willie and Tad.

Bob, Willie, and Tad were friendly boys. The neighbors' children liked to come to their house. The youngsters played circus in the barn and soldier in the yard. They raced through the house in games of "Chase-Me." Mary and her husband did not mind the noise.

"Let the children have a good time," they said.

Often Abraham Lincoln took a group of boys to fish in the Sangamon River. Mary would pack their picnic lunches in big baskets.

"*Sangamon* is an Indian word that means plenty to eat," she told them. "So I have made fried chicken and gingerbread and a great big jar of lemonade!"

Mary was always busy. She cooked and cleaned and sewed. She sewed fancy dresses for herself and shirts for Mr. Lincoln. They were beautiful white shirts with many fine ruffles. Mary loved pretty clothes, and she wanted them for her family as well as for herself.

Sometimes as she sat sewing, her husband stretched out on the floor and read aloud to her. He was so tall that the floor was more comfortable for him than a chair. Usually he read political papers. The Lincolns were still interested in government matters.

Mary still liked parties too. On summer Sundays she often invited a hundred friends home after church for "strawberries and ice cream!"

The little brown house did not really have enough room for such parties. The family needed more room too. One day Mary had an idea.

"I'll surprise Mr. Lincoln the next time he goes away," she thought.

Like many lawyers in Springfield, Abraham Lincoln handled law cases in faraway towns. Sometimes he had to be away from home for several months.

One night when he was away, Mary told her boys, "Tomorrow we are going to raise the roof."

"You mean we'll lift it right off the house?" Bob asked.

"We can't," Willie said. "It's nailed on."

"If we don't have a roof, the rain will fall on me," little Tad cried. "I'll get wet."

Mary laughed. "People raise their roofs to make their homes larger. We will add a second story with five bedrooms upstairs, then put a new roof on top. I hope we can finish it before your father comes home."

The workmen came every day for weeks. They sawed and hammered and painted.

Mary made new curtains for the windows. She

The Lincolns' home in Springfield, after Mary "raised the roof"

bought a black couch for the parlor. It was long enough so that her husband could stretch out on it and be comfortable. She polished the floors and had the bedroom furniture moved upstairs. The boys helped her.

But would Abraham Lincoln like what they were doing? Would he think they had spent too much money? Nobody knew.

At last the house was finished, and just in time! About sunset that evening Willie looked out a parlor window.

"Here comes pa!" he shouted.

Mary hurried to the front door. Bob, Willie, and Tad peeked from behind the window curtains. What would pa do?

Down the street walked Abraham Lincoln. Neighbors came out on their porches to watch. They, too, wanted to see what he would do when he saw how his house had changed.

He reached the corner. He looked up at the tall handsome house. Did he see a parlor curtain move? Did he see three laughing boys peeking from the window? If he did, he made no sign. Instead he turned toward the neighbors on their porches. In a loud voice he called, "Excuse me, friends, but I'm Abe Lincoln and I'm looking for my house. I thought it was on this corner. When I went away a few weeks ago, there was only a one-story house here, and this house has two. I think I must be lost."

With a whoop the boys raced to the door.

"You're not lost, pa!" they shouted.

The neighbors were laughing and so was Mary.

"Welcome home, Mr. Lincoln," she cried.

Abraham Lincoln was laughing too as he hurried up the walk. Everybody could see that he liked his house.

6. Days to Remember

Bands played. Bells rang. A crowd of 6,000 people filled the town square of Alton, Illinois.

"Hurrah for the Little Giant!" some shouted.

"Hurrah for good Old Abe, the Giant Killer!" others cried.

Mary and Bob stood by a flag-draped speaker's stand.

"My goodness!" Mary exclaimed. "All this noise will drive your father's speech right out of his head."

Bob laughed. He was fifteen now, and he had come with his mother from Springfield to this political meeting. They had left Willie and Tad back home with neighbors.

Abraham Lincoln sat on the stand beside the man he was running against for the United States

Senate. The man was Stephen A. Douglas, Mary's old beau! Mr. Douglas was already a famous Illinois senator. Now he was trying to win reelection. People called him the "Little Giant" because of his small size.

During this 1858 campaign the two candidates had often appeared together at meetings.

They debated a question that was tearing the country apart. "Debate" means to talk over, with each speaker taking a different side of the issue. The South believed in slavery. Much of the North did not. The question was whether new states joining the Union should be slave or free. If the trouble was not soon settled, it could lead to civil war.

So what the candidates said in this campaign was important. Newspapers all over the nation reported the Lincoln-Douglas debates. Today was the last one.

Mr. Douglas spoke first. He was a handsome and well-dressed man. He said the South had always had slaves. He believed in "state's rights." That meant that each new state should decide for itself if it would have slavery.

"Let the people rule!" he cried.

It was a good speech. Mary knew that he had made many in the crowd believe as he did.

Mary watched with love and pride as her

husband rose to speak. His coat was wrinkled. As usual, his hair had not stayed combed.

"Some people may not think him handsome," she whispered to Bob. "But his heart is as big as his arms are long."

Abraham Lincoln said that slavery was wrong. Even though the South had always had slaves, that did not make slavery right.

He believed that slavery was like a fire. If it were kept from spreading to new states, it would burn itself out in time.

"Did pa win the debate?" Willie and Tad asked when their parents got home.

"We'll know by the votes on election day," Mary answered.

Election day was gray and wet.

"It will be hard for the farmers to get to the voting places," a worried Mary said that morning. "Their wagons will get stuck in the mud." She knew that her husband counted on the votes of the farm people.

"Perhaps the sun will come out and dry the roads," Bob said.

The sun did not come out. All day the sky was dark, and a cold rain fell on Illinois. Douglas was reelected.

Mary refused to be downhearted. "You'll win next time," she told her husband.

He smiled. "You never give up, do you, Mary?" He called her "Mary" now, but she still called him "Mr. Lincoln."

"You'll see, Mr. Lincoln. Even though you lost, you were right in what you said. People will not forget you," Mary said.

It was true. Many people remembered Abraham Lincoln. In 1860 he was chosen to be the Republican candidate for president. Stephen A. Douglas was a Democratic candidate.

What excitement there was in the Lincolns' house! "Hurrah for Old Abe!" shouted Willie and Tad, now ten and eight.

Suddenly Mary found herself very busy. Many important politicians visited Springfield to see Abraham Lincoln. Newspaper reporters from far away came to write stories about him and his family. Artists arrived to paint his picture.

Mary was up early every morning cleaning her house. She dressed herself and the little boys carefully. Then she baked a yellow cake she called "Election Cake." It was for the visitors and well-wishers who came almost every day. Sometimes by evening guests were seated in every chair in the parlor!

All Springfield was in an uproar. There were speeches and fireworks. There were parades past the Lincolns' house.

A noisy political parade pauses for a moment in front of the Lincolns' home.

Mary and the boys watched the parades from the upstairs windows. Bands played. At night the marchers held burning torches. In one parade there were 6,000 people. It took almost three hours for them all to pass the house.

Yet nobody could really be sure that Abraham Lincoln would be elected president.

Election day came.

Mr. Lincoln spent the day at the State House. Mary stayed at home. It was a worried time for both of them. Waiting for news is hard. By night Mary was very tired.

"Go to bed, Mary," her husband said after supper. "I will stay at the telegraph office. Election news will arrive there. When I learn what has happened, I will come and tell you."

Mary went to bed. It was midnight when Mr. Lincoln came home. He went into the bedroom. By the lamplight he saw Mary sleeping. He touched her shoulder, and she opened her eyes.

"Mary," he said. "Mary, Mary, we are elected!"

7. A Divided Nation

A bright sun shone down on the freshly swept streets of Washington. It was March 4, 1861. Abraham Lincoln had just taken office as the sixteenth president of the United States.

A large wooden platform had been built in front of the Capitol for the inauguration. Green-coated men with guns stood on the roofs of nearby buildings. They were there to guard the new president.

A proud Mary sat on the platform with several hundred people. Her husband was making his first speech as president. All she could see of him was the back of his head. But she could hear his voice as he told the crowd that there must be no war. The North and the South must not break apart into two nations.

"We are not enemies, but friends," he said.

Yet Mary felt that war was near.

Mary's family: Mr. Lincoln and Tad (left); Willie (above left); and Bob (above right).

The South still believed that every state had a right to decide for itself if it would have slavery. If states were not allowed this right, Southerners said they would leave the Union. If the North tried to stop them, they would fight. Already some Southern states were raising money for guns and soldiers.

In his speech Abraham Lincoln appealed to the people to settle the matter peacefully.

Many of the Todd family had come to see the inauguration. The next morning Mary and the Todd ladies looked over the big White House where the nation's presidents lived. The ladies did not like what they saw.

"Everything looks so old and worn," Mary said.

"And dirty too!" her sister Elizabeth exclaimed. "Look at the rugs and wallpaper."

The ladies went up the broad stairs and into a bedroom.

"The best thing in this room is the bed. And it is broken from top to bottom!" Elizabeth said.

Mary looked thoughtful. "The White House should be the finest house in the nation," she said.

"Perhaps Congress will give you money to fix things," Elizabeth told her.

Congress did give the First Lady some money. Mary had the windows washed and the floors polished. She bought beds, chairs, tables, rugs, wallpaper, dishes, and books. She had good taste, and everything she bought was beautiful.

Willie and Tad kept her busy too. They missed their Springfield playmates, and Bob was away studying at Harvard College. Mary learned that two boys lived across the street from the White House—Bud and Holly Taft. She wrote their mother a note inviting the boys over.

Bud was about Willie's age, and Holly was Tad's age. Soon the four were friends and were together often.

The boys ran through the White House shouting and laughing. They wrestled with the president or sat at his knees while he told them a story. They took Tad and Willie's two pet goats and hitched them to a kitchen chair. Then they drove the goats and the chair through the great East Room, where White House parties were held.

Down the long room the four boys raced—*clippety-clop*—and then back again—*lickety-lop*. The little goats pranced, and the boys shouted, "Giddap!" Overhead the crystal lamps shook and rattled.

President and Mrs. Lincoln liked to watch the children at play. It made their dark days brighter, for war had come to the nation.

In February seven of the Southern states had left the Union. They called their new nation the Confederate States of America. Soon the rest of the Southern states joined them. President Lincoln said that the United States could not be split in half. He called for an army of 75,000 Northern troops to fight to save the Union.

Now soldiers were camped on the White House grounds. More army tents stood on the banks of the Potomac River, which flowed past Washington. When soldiers marched to the beat of drums, the little boys thought it exciting. But Mary knew it was very sad.

On a hot July morning, Mary awoke to the sound of heavy guns.

She ran to a window. Across the river lay the

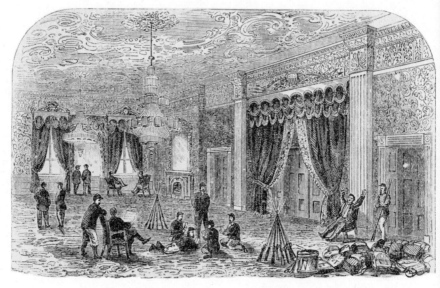

The Civil War became a part of Mary's everyday life
when troops were quartered in the White House.

green fields of Virginia, a Southern state. A great
battle was going on there. It lasted all day. Mary
stood at the window often, trying to see and hear.

People in Washington told one another, "The
North will win this battle, and the war will soon
be over."

Evening brought them bad news. The North had
lost at the Battle of Bull Run. Now everyone knew
it might be a long war.

It was believed the South might attack the
capital. General Scott told the president that his
family should be sent to a safer place.

"Will you go with us?" Mary asked her husband.

He shook his head. "I will not leave Washington at this time."

"Then I will not leave you at this time," Mary said.

The war dragged on. Christmas came. Bob arrived home for a Christmas visit.

"It is wonderful to have the family together again," Mary said.

In the evenings the Lincolns sat around the fireplace. They ate apples and nuts and told Bob all that had happened to them while he was away.

"Bob, you should have seen the big party ma and pa had in honor of Prince Napoleon of France," Tad said. "Napoleon looked grand with a red sash across his chest."

"Pa looked pretty plain in his black suit. But ma was dressed up, you bet," Willie said.

"I'll bet," Bob laughed.

His mother and father laughed too.

It was a good Christmas for the family in the White House.

8. The White House

Mary tried to smile as she talked to her guests. But upstairs in the White House, Willie lay sick.

Downstairs the president and his wife were giving a party. They had 500 guests. Some were listening to the music of the Marine Band. Some were eating the fine supper laid out in the state dining room—turkey, duck, ham, fruit. A few were telling Mary how pretty she looked. She had on a new white dress with a long train that lay on the floor behind her.

Before the party the president had looked at that train and smiled. "My, what a long tail our cat has tonight!"

Now as the party went on, Mary worried and watched for a chance to slip away from her guests. At last it came. She hurried up the stairs to Willie's room. He was asleep.

Mary felt his hot cheeks and grew more worried. She wished there were no party in the White House tonight. Slowly she went back down the stairs.

In the next days, Willie's fever grew worse. Then Tad became ill with the same kind of fever. Mary sat beside their beds day and night.

One sad morning the doctor told the Lincolns that Willie could not get well. Bob came home from college to be with his family. Only Bob stood beside his heartbroken father in the East Room during Willie's funeral. Tad was still sick. Mary was in bed, too, ill from grief.

It took a long time for Tad to get well and even longer for Mary. Her family was the most important thing in the world to Mary. Losing Willie was almost more than she could bear.

By the time she was well, Bud and Holly Taft had gone away to school. No longer were there four laughing boys to scamper through the White House. Only Tad was left.

With Tad beside her, Mary visited wounded soldiers in the hospitals. She took them lemons and oranges. She always had time to stop at each bed and talk to each lonely soldier. Comforting them helped to comfort her own aching heart.

The soldiers all liked the First Lady. They saw that she was kind. But there were people who did not like her.

These were political enemies of the president. They hoped to harm him through his wife. From Mary's first days in Washington, they had found fault with her.

"She is a nobody from a country town in the West," they said. "She will not know how to be a First Lady."

Soon they saw that Mary did know how to care for the White House and to give the parties that were part of a president's job. She dressed nicely. She was smart and could discuss politics. She even spoke French with visitors from France.

So they said, "She is too interested in clothes and parties. She spends too much money on the White House. She tries to meddle in political matters. She has a sharp tongue."

They found fault with President Lincoln too, and especially when he signed the Emancipation Proclamation. This was the famous paper that said the slaves in the South could be free.

Some of the things people said about Mary were true. She did love clothes and parties. And she had spent more money on the White House than Congress had given her. The president said he would pay Mary's extra bills from his own pocket. He knew she had only wanted to make the White House beautiful.

Quick-tempered Mary talked back sharply to those who found fault with her. That made more enemies for the president. Then Mary was sorry, and she tried to make up with the people. Few of them understood that beneath her quick hot words lay a good heart.

Most of the ugly things that people said about Mary were untrue. The worst was that she was a traitor to the North! They knew that her family, the Todds, lived in Kentucky, where many people sided with the South.

"Mary's brothers are fighting for the South," people said. "She wants the South to win."

Mary always wore beautiful gowns to White House balls and receptions.

"Why should I want the rebels to win?" Mary exclaimed fiercely. "They would hang my husband tomorrow if they could."

Some of Mary's brothers did fight for the South. Three of them were killed. Mary had loved them, but she dared not let people see her grief. She could only cry into her pillow at night. They were the tears of a sister, not a traitor.

Sometimes in the dark nights Mary cried for the president too. The long war had been hard on him. Often he was too busy to eat or rest. He grew very thin and tired. When Mary saw him working at his desk late into the night, she worried about his health. She was also worried for his safety. Once he was shot at when he was riding on horseback to the Soldiers' Home. The bullet went through his tall stovepipe hat.

The war was almost three years old when Mary's youngest sister, Emilie, visited the White House. It was December 1863.

Emilie did not look like the pretty child who had thought Abraham Lincoln was a giant, nor the lovely girl who had often visited the Lincolns in Springfield. She was pale and sad. Her young husband had just been killed fighting for the South.

Now in the White House the Lincolns hugged the youngest Todd sister. They wanted to comfort her.

"You must stay with us as long as you can, little sister," the president said.

But at once people began to say that the Lincolns had an "enemy" from the South in the White House.

Emilie saw that she was causing trouble. So she said that she must leave. Sadly the president and Mary told her good-bye. She had been with them for only a week.

The terrible war was not only breaking the nation apart. It was breaking families apart too.

9. Assassination!

April sunshine lighted the White House windows. Around the breakfast table sat the president and Mrs. Lincoln, Bob, and Tad.

There was a look of happiness on every face. After four long years the North had won the Civil War. Now the Union was saved and the slaves were free.

Bob was a grown man now. He had just come safely home from the fighting. After finishing college he had joined the army. Mary looked at him proudly.

"I've brought you a present, pa," Bob said. He held out a little picture of the great Southern general, Robert E. Lee.

The president looked carefully at General Lee's picture.

"It is the face of a noble, brave man," he said. "Soon we shall live in peace with all the brave men who have been fighting us. We can all be cheerful again."

Mary said, "You and I will begin by going to Ford's Theater tonight. There is a funny play."

That night the Lincolns rode in their carriage over the cobblestone streets to the theater. Clouds hid the moon, and the wind was sharp. But Mary felt secure and warm beside her husband. She

The assassination of Abraham Lincoln

remembered a conversation they'd had earlier in the day.

"After I leave office, I want to take you and Tad to Europe," the president had told her. He still had four more years as president, for he had been elected to a second term. Mary had not seen her husband so happy in a long time.

"Everything is going to be better from now on," she thought as they drew up in front of the theater.

Inside the theater people stood and clapped for the president. The Lincolns took their seats in a flag-draped box at one side of the stage.

The theater lights were dimmed. On the stage the actors began to speak their lines. Soon the audience was laughing.

In their dark box, the president reached out and took Mary's hand. So they sat, holding hands and laughing. They did not hear a man creep into the back of the box.

Suddenly a shot rang out. The president fell forward in his chair, a great wound in the back of his head. The gunman jumped down on the stage and ran off.

For a moment Mary did not know what had happened. Then she screamed, "The president is shot!"

After that, everything was noise and confusion in Ford's Theater. Men carried the president to a bedroom in a house across the street. He was too badly wounded for the long trip back to the White House. People said that the gunman had been John Wilkes Booth, a Southern actor.

For the rest of the night, Mary sat in the little parlor of the borrowed house. Friends came to be with her. Bob came and stood beside his father's bed. Doctors came—sixteen in all. They did what they could for the president, but they knew that he could not be saved. Vice-President Andrew Johnson came. Tomorrow he would be the new president.

At times through the night, Mary went to her husband's bedside. It was a small wooden bed and too short for the president. His feet hung over the side. He did not look wounded but only as if he were sleeping. Mary knelt beside him and wept.

In the morning rain beat against the windows.

Bob came to Mary. "Pa is gone," he said.

He led her to Abraham Lincoln's side. A wild grief swept over Mary. She threw herself across her husband's body.

"Oh, why did you not tell me he was dying!" she cried.

Bob took his mother outside to a waiting carriage. Church bells were tolling. It was raining hard, as though the sky itself wept on that morning of April 15, 1865.

Mary looked across the street at the dark brick front of Ford's Theater. "Oh, that dreadful house! That dreadful house!" she said.

After Abraham Lincoln's funeral, a grieving Mary and her sons left the White House and moved to Chicago. Mary never lived in Washington again. She missed her husband too much. She knew that in Washington she would feel even sadder without him.

For a long while Mary and Tad traveled in Europe, just as Mr. Lincoln had planned they should all do together. Then when Tad was eighteen, he died of a lung disease. To Mary, this was the final blow. Her health failed, and for many years she was ill.

Mary never got over the loss of her husband. But as time went by, she did find some happiness in the way the nation loved and honored his memory.

Finally Mary went back to Springfield to live with her sister Elizabeth.

On a golden summer evening she died in that same house where she and Abraham Lincoln had been married so many years before. She was 63. On her finger she still wore the ring that said: "Love is eternal."

Index

C.1